THE GREAT TEA ROOMS OF AMERICA

THE GREAT TEA ROOMS OF AMERICA

Text and photographs by
Bruce Richardson

BENJAMIN PRESS

Other books by Bruce & Shelley Richardson:
A Year of Teas at the Elmwood Inn
A Tea for All Seasons
The Tea Table
The New Tea Companion
The Great Tea Rooms of Britain
Looking Deeply Into Tea
Tea in the City: New York
Tea in the City: London

Third Edition © 2006 by Bruce Richardson
Second Edition © 2003 by Bruce Richardson
Copyright © 2002 Bruce Richardson
Photographs Copyright © 2002, 2003, 2006 by Bruce Richardson
Photo editor: Benjamin Richardson
Additional photographs courtesy of Butchart Gardens (page 19, 20, 21-A),
The Drake Hotel (page 30-B, 31),
Pages 58-61 used by permission of Disney Enterprises, Inc.

BENJAMIN PRESS
P. O. Box 100
Perryville, Kentucky 40468 USA
800.765.2139
www.benjaminpress.com

ISBN 0-9663478-6-2

Printed in China

Acknowledgements

Choosing the tea rooms to go into this collection has been a daunting task. Master Tea Blender John Harney suggested I do this book shortly after I published the first edition of *The Great Tea Rooms of Britain*. I told him then that I doubted there were enough tea rooms in America to justify a book. That changed dramatically over the past decade as hundreds of tea rooms sprang up coast to coast. That vital resurgence of interest in tea rooms brought a number of distinguished venues to the forefront of America's tea culture.

The second challenge in producing this book was the task of travelling great distances to visit tea rooms. Researching my British book was easily accomplished by driving across England, Scotland, and Wales in three trips totaling 25 days. Often my photographer and I would cruise the countryside hoping to stumble upon a remarkable tea room in some remote village. This was not possible in America. Preparing the first edition included 12 tours, nearly 100,000 air miles, numerous trains, and countless rental cars in a three year span. I once visited six Southern California tea rooms in 48 hours and had tea and scones in each! With this third edition, four new tea rooms have been added and several have been removed, mainly due to closings.

I met hospitable hosts at every stop. They took time from their busy schedules to prepare food shots. They sat down over a cup of tea to talk about how hard they worked. They even cleaned up the occasional broken teacup knocked over by my gangly tripods. Tea room owners are the most accommodating and gracious people you will ever meet. I'm sure that's why they are in the tea business.

Throughout this project I have received suggestions from people who wanted their favorite tea room included. Some tea room owners and friends called asking if they were going to be in the book. Unfortunately, I couldn't investigate and photograph every location brought to my attention. This is by no means a "top tea room" list. My aim is to give readers an overview of different tea room styles represented across the country. My selections have been confirmed by countless conversations I have had with professionals in the tea trade and, in large part, through comments from the readers of my books.

There will be opportunities for additional inclusions in future editions so please contact me with any suggestions. For a complete listing of tea rooms in America, visit www.catteacorner.com.

My thanks go to my editor, Freear Williams. My son, Ben served as my photographer's assistant, traveling partner, and photo editor. Guidance and assistance also came from Pearl Dexter, publisher of *TEA Magazine* and Troy Segal, senior editor at *Zagat Survey*. My sincerest gratitude goes to my loyal readers who use my books as they travel the world with tea on their minds.

Bruce Richardson

Rose Tree Cottage, Pasadena, California

THE GREAT TEA ROOMS OF AMERICA

Introduction

Americans have a great affection for tea. The ancient beverage and all its trappings may not be as ingrained in our social habits as in Great Britain or China, but it has played a defining role in shaping the culture and politics of our young nation.

America's love affair with tea was born from her British and Dutch heritages. William Penn introduced tea drinking to the Quaker colony that he founded in Delaware in 1682. Within a few years, the arriving immigrants brought with them tea rituals that had been a part of the cultures in their homelands. By 1757, tea had become such a vital part of society that Manhattan established special "tea water pumps" and the City of New York enacted a law for "the tea water men."

The love of tea was so great that, in the years leading up to the Revolution, the per capita consumption of tea in America was greater than in England. The problem was that all tea brought into the colonies passed through English hands and was heavily taxed by King George II. "The women of the colonies will pay any price for their beloved tea," he is rumored to have said. King George's tax scheme failed and the women revolted. Patriotic fervor spread down the eastern seaboard and indignant women signed pledges to never again drink the King's tea. They didn't go as far as to forgo the ritual of teatime, they simply replaced the tea leaves with local herbs and infusions such as sassafras or raspberry vine.

The young ladies of Boston signed a pledge stating, "We the daughters of those patriots who have, and do now appear for the public interest, and in that principally regard their posterity, as such do with pleasure engage with them in denying ourselves the drinking of foreign tea, in hopes to frustrate a plan that tends to deprive a whole community of all that is valuable to life."

The following verses enjoyed a wide circulation:

A Lady's Adieu to Her Tea-Table
FAREWELL the Tea-board with your gaudy attire,
Ye cups and ye saucers that I did admire;
To my cream pot and tongs I now bid adieu
That pleasure's all fled that I once found in you.
Farewell pretty chest that so lately did shine,
With hyson and congo and best double fine;
Many a sweet moment by you I have sat,
Hearing girls and old maids to tattle and chat;
And the spruce coxcomb laugh at nothing at all,
Only some silly work that might happen to fall.
No more shall my teapot so generous be
In filling the cups with this pernicious tea,
For I'll fill it with water and drink out the same,
Before I'll lose LIBERTY that dearest name,
Because I am taught (and believe it is fact)
That our ruin is aimed at in the late act,
Of imposing a duty on all foreign Teas,
Which detestable stuff we can quit when we please.
LIBERTY'S The Goddess that I do adore,
And I'll maintain her right until my last hour,
Before she shall part I will die in the cause,
For I'll never be govern'd by tyranny's laws.

Independence fever swelled to the boiling point on the evening of December 16, 1773 when the sailing ship *Dartmouth* was boarded by irate citizens in Boston Harbor. Dressed as Mohawk Indians, they took only three hours to empty the contents of 342 chests of tea leaves into the seawater. The Boston Tea Party was one of several tea uprisings that took place in major ports along the coast.

Following the Revolutionary War, America staked its own claim in the tea trade, thanks in large part to the development of fast-sailing tea ships

MacNab's Tea Room, Boothbay, Maine

modeled after the Baltimore clippers. These American marvels made the arduous trip to China and back in only 180 days. By the turn of the twentieth century, tea had become a source of social congregation. In both America and England, fine hotels housed tea courts and tea rooms where men and women could gather in the late afternoon, sip tea, and exchange pleasantries. These tea rooms and tea courts soon moved to host tea dances, where spirits soared over the freedom and conveniences afforded by the ever evolving technology of the day.

When you ask someone to describe an American tea room today you will likely get a variety of answers. A tea room in Alabama means something different than a tea room in British Columbia. A hotel tea in New York might have little resemblance to an Asian tea room in Washington, D.C. Much of what America knows about tea rooms came about in the 1920's and 30's when we became a nation on wheels. As people became mobile, small restaurants and cafes sprang up along the highways to feed the growing number of tourists. Many of these privately owned eateries were owned and operated by women who had well-honed skills in cooking and hospitality. They had spent much of their lives cooking for large families and countless church suppers. They would sometimes renovate rundown buildings or cottages and give them a charming low-budget decorating scheme using readily-available furnishings and fabrics. The dining rooms were decorated in a feminine style to appeal to the women who were traveling in great numbers. One drawback was that these frilly female sanctuaries were not always alluring to businessmen. Duncan Hines once said that "men's phobia about tea rooms makes them miss a lot of good eating."

The simple menus included home cooked items such as chicken salad or baked ham that were perfect for a light luncheon. The highlight of the meal was the homemade breads or rich desserts. The drink of choice was usually tea - cold, not hot. This type of establishment is still common across the southern United States. A recent directory of tea rooms in Texas lists 160 such establishments. It would be difficult to find a hot cup of loose tea and an English scone in many of them but, without a doubt, most will offer a version of chicken salad and iced tea.

Earlier in the century, two serendipitous discoveries were made leading to the proliferation

Dunbar Tea Room, Sandwich, Massachusetts

of iced tea. In 1904, Richard Blechynden, a tea vendor at the World's Fair in St. Louis, weary of selling his cups of hot tea in the summer heat, dropped ice in the beverage in an attempt to boost sales. His gimmick worked. The result was the first iced tea. A second invention occurred in 1908 when Thomas Sullivan began to ship tea samples in individual bags to New York restaurants. He found that restaurants were preparing the tea samples without extracting the tea from the bag. Hence, bagged tea was born, allowing a tea drinker to effortlessly produce a hot cup of tea on demand.

One of America's top ten tea rooms during the 1930's was the McDonald's Tea Room in Gallatin, Missouri (not related to the golden arches found today). Virginia McDonald's fame and baking prowess was spread by news media across the country, including *The Saturday Evening Post*. Her advice for young brides? "I think any girl who really is interested in making a success of her marriage should learn to be a good cook," she said.

An interesting offshoot of this boom in tea rooms was the appearance of cooking schools devoted to tea room management. One of the largest was the Tea Room Institute of Washington, D.C., founded in 1916. These culinary entrepreneurs offered a convenient home study program entitled "Pouring Tea for Profit" that promised graduates the opportunity to make the incredible sum of $35 to $50 per week as a tea room manager. The position was described as "a pleasant, dignified, enjoyable profession that gives you an enviable social position in the community and commands the respect and admiration of all who know you."

Following a post World War II decline in the consumption of tea, America rediscovered the ancient beverage in the 1990's. The number of tea rooms and sales of gourmet teas began to grow steadily as more and more tea companies entered the market. Tea room seminars, tea books and tea conferences now are popular topics at any gourmet food show. Over 125 tea companies may be found in the United States and Canada.

Many Americans had their first taste of well-made tea overseas. They enjoyed tea at hotels such as The Ritz in London or The Peninsula in Hong Kong. Upon returning home, they sought out tea rooms and tea shops that allowed them to recreate that satisfying and refined teatime tradition.

Leading this second American Tea Revolution are a number of outstanding tea venues in Canada and the United States where the art of tea is taken to greater heights. The emphasis here is on the celebration of afternoon tea, that elegant multi-coursed mid-afternoon affair first brought to life by the British. Not to be confused with *high tea* (a common English supper taken with a pot of tea at a high dining table), this event is aimed first at satisfying the spirit, then the appetite.

One refreshing aspect of American tea rooms is the eclectic mix of cuisines from which tea room chefs choose. No longer confined to the traditional egg salad or cucumber sandwiches, American tea rooms offer a wide variety of savory and sweet selections drawing on traditions from all parts of the world. The recipes found in this collection are indicative of the vast array of delicious foods available to modern tea room patrons.

Guests now choose from tea lists that resemble wine lists at fine restaurants. The standard offerings of English Breakfast and Earl Grey have been joined by First and Second Flush Darjeelings, green teas, white teas, oolongs and herbals. Tea customers are becoming sophisticated in their choosing thanks to articles about tea that regularly appear in magazines and newspapers.

As is the case in Britain, American tea rooms are found in myriad locations. Besides the grand hotels in major cities, tea is being served in cozy inns, B & B's, restored mansions, farm houses and cottages. The tea locations found in this book cater not just to women, but also to men. One hotel tea even offers a hearty tea menu aimed at a man's appetite. Tea room owners are realizing that to be successful, they need to create an inviting environment where men feel equally comfortable.

Most of all, the popularity of afternoon tea can be linked to the fact that Americans are looking for a respite from fast food, cell phones and abrupt service. At an outstanding tea room, the pace should be relaxed, the surroundings serene, and the service attentive. The customer should leave with his/her soul refreshed - much like exiting a church service. A great tea room is not just a restaurant, it is a sanctuary from our fast-paced society.

"There is a great deal of poetry and fine sentiment in a chest of tea."

Ralph Waldo Emerson

Disney's Grand Floridian Resort & Spa

Swan House, Findlay, Ohio

THE GREAT TEA ROOMS OF AMERICA

TABLE OF CONTENTS

THE BROWN PALACE

Denver, Colorado

The story of the Brown Palace Hotel begins in a setting ripe for entrepreneurship. It was the late 1800s in Denver, Colorado and people from all over the country were still flocking to the west, seeking fortunes in gold and silver. Everyone stopped in Denver, either on their way to or from the mountains. Some settled, some moved on, but all needed a place to stay.

Henry Cordes Brown, a former carpenter from Ohio, came to Denver in 1860 to purchase several acres of land, including a triangular plot at the corners of Broadway, Tremont and 17th Streets where he grazed cattle. Brown made a name for himself by donating land for the state capitol building and by contributing the first $1000 to build the city's first library. He then decided what Denver really needed was a grand hotel and that he would build it.

Work began in 1888 on the Italian Renaissance building, using Colorado red granite and Arizona sandstone for the building's exterior. Inside, architect Frank Edbrooke designed the country's first atrium lobby with balconies rising eight floors above ground, surrounded by cast iron railings with ornate grillwork panels. The hotel was hailed as the second fire-proof building in America. No wood was used for the floors and walls.

After a construction expenditure of $1.6 million, remarkable for the time, and another $400,000 for furniture, the Brown Palace opened on August 12, 1892. It has remained open every minute since then, even during a recent $6.5 million restoration of the top two floors.

The tradition of "taking tea" at the Brown Palace is a long-standing one; guests have been doing it for over a century. Today, afternoon tea is served daily in the midst of the atrium lobby, accompanied by either a harpist or pianist.

Specially commissioned Royal Doulton bone china graces each tea table, along with engraved silver tea pots. Every detail has been considered, down to the silver tea strainers.

Scones, tea pastries and beautiful tea sandwiches are artfully prepared by the hotel's culinary staff each day. Devonshire cream is shipped directly from England. Uniformed wait staff, schooled in the art of English tea service, look after every need. Guests choose between the traditional Brown's Tea or the Royale Palace Tea. In addition, Luncheon Tea with a selection of four entrée salads is offered from noon until 2:00.

Afternoon Tea in this grand space has had some unusual accompaniments over the past century. Because of its long standing association with the National Western Stock Show, the Brown Palace has a tradition of displaying champion steers and bulls in the atrium lobby during teatime each January.

Cowboy star Monty Montana used to ride his horse, Rex, into the hotel, usually roping the general manager. On at least one occasion, Monty rode Rex up the grand staircase to a meeting of the Rodeo Cowboys Association.

A visit to Denver affords travelers opportunity to see a variety of unique sites. The Rocky Mountains are outside your window. The internationally recognized Denver Art Museum and Coors Field, home of the Colorado Rockies Baseball Club, are both a short walk away. The impressive Denver Mint stands further south. A free tour of this fascinating operation is sure to be one of the highlights of any visit to the mile-high city.

Standing the test of time, the Brown Palace today remains what it was originally meant to be: a grand, unprecedented hotel framed by the grandeur of one of North America's supreme mountain ranges. Indeed, the Brown Palace is still known for many of its original qualities — its unusual shape, stunning eight story atrium lobby, elegant atmosphere, and perhaps most importantly, the ability to treat guests like royalty.

Baby Cakes

2/3 cup	butter, room temperature
1 3/4 cups	sugar
2	eggs
2 teaspoons	vanilla extract
3 cups	cake flour
2 teaspoons	baking powder
3/4 teaspoon	salt
1 1/4 cups	milk
	slightly sweetened whipped cream
	fresh fruit, such as berries or kiwi

Preheat oven to 325° F. Wash and dry 14 tin cans, 14 to 16 ounces each, or 14 small (1-cup) soufflé dishes; grease and flour insides.

In large bowl of electric mixer, beat butter, sugar, eggs, and vanilla until fluffy. Beat 5 minutes on high speed, scraping bowl occasionally.

Combine flour, baking powder, and salt. Add dry ingredients to batter alternately with milk. Spoon about 1/3 cup of batter into each prepared tin can. Bake until a toothpick inserted in center comes out clean, 25 to 30 minutes.

Remove to a wire rack and cool completely, until the edges become dry and crusty. Run a knife around the inside of cans or dishes to loosen edges, tap on a counter, then turn cakes out.

With a serrated knife, cut off and discard the rounded tops of cakes. Turn cakes upside down so cut edges are on the bottom. Cut cakes into two layers and fill with whipped cream and fresh fruit.

For a fun presentation, use pinking shears to cut out squares of colorful wrapping paper large enough to cover the center of your dessert places. Serve the Baby Cakes on the wrapping-paper.

Chocolate Truffle Cups

6 ounces   semisweet chocolate chips

Melt chocolate in a double boiler or a bowl set over a pan of hot water. Stir until smooth.

Working quickly, use the back of a spoon or a small knife to spread chocolate on bottom and up sides of 7 to 8 paper cupcake liners. Set liners in a muffin pan. Chill until firm in freezer, 10-15 minutes.

Carefully peel off the paper liners, handling chocolate as little as possible. (May be kept refrigerated for up to 5 days.)

Mousse Filling

1 1/3 cups	whipping cream
2/3 cup	confectioner's sugar, sifted
1/3 cup	Dutch-process cocoa, sifted
1 teaspoon	powdered instant coffee (not granules)
2 teaspoons	dark rum (optional)
	confectioners' sugar or cocoa for decoration

Place cream, sugar, cocoa, instant coffee, and rum (if used) in large mixing bowl. Beat with electric mixer or whisk until cream forms soft peaks but is not stiff. Adjust flavoring to taste.

Spoon into small chocolate truffle cups and refrigerate until serving. Decorate tops with a dusting of confectioners' sugar or cocoa, if desired, just before serving.

Double Chocolate Brownies

1 1/4 cups	all-purpose flour
1/4 teaspoon	soda
1/4 teaspoon	salt
1/2 cup	butter
2 cups	semi-sweet chocolate chips
3	eggs
1 teaspoon	vanilla
1 cup	sugar
1/3 cup	chopped nuts

Preheat oven to 350° F. Grease a 13x9x2-inch baking pan. Combine flour, soda, and salt.

In a large saucpan over low heat, melt butter and half the chocolate chips, stirring until smooth. Remove from heat and allow to cool.

Stir in remaining chips and nuts. Spread into prepared pan. Bake 18-22 minutes. Cool completely. Cut into 24 brownies

BUTCHART GARDENS

Victoria, British Columbia

In 1904, Robert Butchart began manufacturing Portland Cement at Tod Inlet on Vancouver Island, 21 miles north of Victoria. In 1904, he and his family established their home there. As he exhausted the limestone in the quarry near their house, his enterprising wife, Jenny, conceived an unprecedented plan for refurbishing the bleak pit that resulted. She requisitioned tons of top soil from farmland nearby, had it brought to Tod Inlet by horse and cart, and used it to line the floor of the abandoned quarry. With the help of her husband's workers, and under her personal supervision, the abandoned quarry bloomed as the spectacular Sunken Garden.

The plant stopped manufacturing cement in 1916, but continued to make tiles and flower pots as late as 1950. A single kiln chimney now overlooks the quarry Mrs. Butchart so miraculously reclaimed.

Mr. Butchart took great pride in his wife's remarkable work. He collected ornamental birds amongst her ravishing flowers; trained pigeons at the site of the present Begonia Bower; ducks in the Star Pond; noisy peacocks on the front lawn; and a curmudgeon of a parrot in the main house. By 1908, reflecting their own world travels, the Butcharts had created a Japanese Garden on the sea-side of their home, and later constructed a symmetrical Italian Garden on the site of their former tennis court.

The renown of Mrs. Butchart's gardening quickly spread. By the 1920's, more than 50,000 people came each year to see her creation. She was a generous hostess, not only to her own friends but to hundreds of visitors to Victoria. In appreciation of her generosity, in 1931 she was named Victoria's best citizen. Between them, Jennie and Robert Butchart seemed to come up with a magical formula that brought many people great happiness. In a gesture toward all their visitors, the hospitable Butcharts christened their estate "Benvenuto," the Italian word for "Welcome."

Their house grew into a comfortable, luxurious showplace, with a bowling alley, indoor salt-water swimming pool, paneled billiard room and - wonder of its age! - a self-playing Aeolian pipe organ. Today the residence contains the Dining Room Restaurant, offices, and rooms still used for private entertaining.

The Butchart Gardens has grown to be the premier West Coast display garden, while maintaining the gracious traditions of the past. Over one million people visit each year, enjoying the floral beauty, entertainment and lighting programs.

The Butchart Gardens today has established an international reputation for continuously flowering plants. Each year over one million bedding plants are used throughout the Gardens to ensure uninterrupted bloom from March through October.

The custom of serving tea was started by Jennie Butchart in the early 1900's, making the Gardens host to Victoria's oldest and best-loved tea tradition. In the spirit of the founders' hospitality, both afternoon and high teas are served year-round in the original Butchart home and seasonally in the stunning Italian Garden.

Afternoon tea begins with a colorful seasonal fruit cup topped with citrus yogurt cream. A tiered tray of freshly-made tea sandwiches and homemade sweets then follows. Candied ginger scones with berry jam and whipped Devon cream round out the menu. The sandwiches offered are some of the most innovative tea time creations to be found.

The High Tea is a complete meal with the addition of Cornish pasties, salmon rolls, savory herb potato scones and toasted crumpets. The enjoyment of all these beautiful and delicious foods is enhanced by the stunning vistas seen through the Butchart windows. The deep-blue Canadian sky serves as a tranquil backdrop to the innumerable shades of green found in the classic Italian gardens.

"An old garden is like an old friend. As with old friends memories come and certain spots give memories forever dear." This adage is carried out with great detail in the gardens surrounding the former Butchart home. On an island, whose climate and rich soil nurture spectacular floral beauty, guests find the scenery sweetened even more with the addition of an outstanding afternoon tea. It is one of the great memories of a visit to Victoria - both for the eye and the soul.

Roasted Vegetable and Asiago Quiche

2	carrots, peeled
15	mushrooms
1	tomato, quartered
6	garlic cloves
2	red peppers
1	onion
1/2 cup	olive oil
pinch	salt
pinch	black pepper
1 cup	Asiago cheese

Preheat oven to 390° F.

Cut all vegetables into medium dice. Toss with olive oil, salt and pepper. Place in a heat proof dish and roast in oven for 20-30 minutes or until the vegetables are caramelized. Cool vegetables and finely chop.

Quiche Cream

8	eggs, large
1 cup	whipping cream
pinch	nutmeg
12	3" tart shells

Prebake shells according to package directions.

In a bowl, whisk eggs, cream, and nutmeg together. Add grated Asiago cheese. Heat oven to 300° F. Spoon vegetable mix into baked shells and cover with quiche cream. Bake for 10 -15 minutes or until set in the middle.

Candied Ginger Scones

3 cups	all-purpose flour
5 tablespoons	sugar
2/3 pound	cold butter, unsalted
1/2 cup	Australian Candied Ginger
5	eggs, large
1 1/4 cups	2% milk

Preheat oven to 350° F.

Mix dry ingredients and finely chopped candied ginger together. Cut in butter using a pastry cutter until it forms "pea size" balls.

Combine eggs and milk and incorporate into flour mixture. Let rest.

Roll out dough and cut to desired shape. Brush with egg wash or milk and then sprinkle with white sugar. Bake 20 minutes or until golden brown.

Serve scones with whipped Devonshire cream and fresh fruit preserves.

Lemon Poppy Seed Loaf

1/2 pound	butter, unsalted
1 1/2 cups	sugar
2	eggs, large
1 cup	2% milk
2 cups	all-purpose flour
2 teaspoons	baking powder
1 teaspoon	salt
2	lemons, zest only
3 tablespoons	poppy seeds

Preheat oven to 350° F.

Cream butter and sugar together in a bowl.

Add eggs slowly, one at a time. Scrape down the bowl, add dry ingredients and then wet ingredients, scrape the bowl well. Add poppy seeds and lemon zest, mix lightly.

Pour batter in a lightly greased loaf pan and bake for 30-35 minutes or until golden brown. Let cool.

Lemon Syrup

2	lemons, juiced
6 tablespoons	sugar
6 tablespoons	water

In a sauce pan, combine lemon juice, sugar, and water. Reduce over low heat until thick in consistency. Pour over loaves.

CLIFFSIDE INN

Newport, Rhode Island

Newport has long been the retreat of America's rich and famous. The Vanderbilts and Astors knew a good place to put down roots. After all, they developed Palm Beach, the Hudson Valley and the Berkshires for seasonal getaways.

By the 1860's, it was not fashionable to stay at a Newport hotel for the summer season. One must own or rent a cottage. Most of the bigger hotels closed while more cottages were being built. Due to the Civil War, cottagers hailing from New York and Boston dominated summer society. Newport attracted not only America's financial elite, but many of its most gifted artists, writers, educators, scientists, politicians and architects. The day was spent playing croquet, sailing, or listening to band concerts on the lawn.

These summer homes were generally shingle-clad resort architecture inspired by the contemporary British Queen Anne style and American Colonial buildings. By the late 1900's, an entirely different taste took over. Grand new cottages were built in a palatial scale. This rush to opulence, led by families such as the Vanderbilts, made Newport *the* place in America to experience the Gilded Age. William Vanderbilt set the standard for future building in 1892 when he opened Marble House as a gift for his wife, Alva. On fashionable Bellevue Avenue, it was the finest summer house money could buy.

It cost William Vanderbilt $11 million to build and decorate Marble House, but Alva divorced him four years after the project was finished. She got the house, which she closed soon after marrying William's friend and neighbor. When her second husband died, Alva discovered the cause of female suffrage, and reopened Marble House in 1909 to hold benefit teas. Teapots still found in the scullery bear the phrase "Votes for Women." She went so far as to build her own Chinese Teahouse in 1913, overlooking the Cliff Walk next to the sea.

Further down Cliff Walk stands one of Newport's premier inns and a setting for one of New England's finest afternoon teas, The Cliffside Inn.

In a city known for eccentricity, Cliffside Inn was once the home of Newport's most peculiar and mysterious personality, Beatrice Turner.

The wealthy and hauntingly beautiful artist had a reputation as being an eccentric recluse. In the early 1900's, as styles changed, she and her mother continued to dress in Victorian clothes. Following her father's death in 1913, she had her fabulous Newport home painted black. It remained that color for 45 years.

After Beatrice died in 1948, executors of the estate opened the neglected and decaying home to find every room of the three-story mansion piled high with paintings. The vast majority were self-portraits. She painted herself sitting, standing, at home, on the town, in evening gowns, in dressing gowns - and after her mother died she painted herself in the nude.

Unable to sell the paintings, most were burned in a bonfire at the Newport dump. Fortunately, a roguish New York attorney rescued 70 artworks from the fire and took them on tour. The tour was unsuccessful but journalists found the story fascinating. The Hearst newspapers printed the legend of Beatrice Turner in 1949 and *Life* magazine followed with a photo spread in 1950. The paintings then disappeared.

When Winthrop P. Baker acquired Cliffside Inn, he was impressed by the detailed architecture of the house with its Victorian turrets, gabled roof and grand porch. He also was smitten by the 1921 double portrait of Beatrice Turner and her mother hanging in the parlor. His curiosity aroused, the former television journalist soon discovered that the house had once been filled with the images of Beatrice.

Baker has accumulated many paintings by Beatrice through the years. Once again, they fill the halls and adorn every guest room. Many of the larger canvases hang in the parlor where they look down at guests enjoying afternoon tea. His fascination with the Turner story led him to commission and publish a book on the artist's life entitled *Beatrice: The Untold Story of a Legendary Woman of Mystery.*

The ritual of afternoon tea is featured in the diary entries carefully kept by Beatrice. She speaks often of taking tea in both her family home in Philadelphia and her beloved Cliffside.

Baker and his talented staff have turned Cliffside Inn into one of the most celebrated lodgings in Newport. Thirteen guest suites are found in the main house, each completely refurbished with working fireplaces and furnished with elegant antiques. An adjacent cottage contains two more impressive rooms. "Our goal," he relates, "is to make the Cliffside Inn equally, if not better, known for its

afternoon teas." Inspired by Beatrice's love of afternoon tea, the staff has researched and recreated a daily tea event worthy of the Newport tradition.

Each afternoon, a complete array of tea foods are set for the inn's guests. They include strawberry almond tartlets, shortbread, scones with curds and cream, cucumber sandwiches, crab-stuffed mushrooms, angels on horseback, chocolate dipped fruits, assorted French pastries and a selection of hot teas.

Guests may linger as long as they like and enjoy the refreshments to their hearts' and appetites' content. Resting on the Victorian sofas beside the bay window or in the high backed chairs in front of the fireplace makes the event a luxurious respite following a long day traipsing through mansions or shopping in the old town area.

Surely the Vanderbilts, the Astors, and even Beatrice Turner spent many leisurely afternoons enjoying fine "Newport Teas." It is doubtful that any could have been more satisfying or more elegant than the afternoon tea presented today at the Cliffside Inn.

Beatrice Sugar Cookies

1/2 cup	butter, softened
1 cup	powdered sugar
1 teaspoon	vanilla
2	egg yolks
1 1/3 cups	all-purpose flour
1/2 cup	blanched almonds
	powdered sugar for dusting

Cream butter and sugar together in a mixer and add vanilla and egg yolks. Mix in flour and blanched almonds. Form into a ball. Refrigerate dough for 20 minutes.

Preheat oven to 350° F. Roll dough on a floured surface to desired thickness. Cut dough with a heart-shaped cookie cutter and place on un-greased cookie sheet. Bake for 12-15 minutes. Allow cookies to cool on baking sheet for only 5 minutes and then remove to a cooling rack. Dust with powdered sugar before serving.

Ahrens Tea Cake

1/2 cup	butter
1 cup	sugar
2	eggs
2 teaspoons	vanilla
2 cups	all-purpose flour
2 teaspoons	baking powder
1 teaspoon	baking soda
1 cup	sour cream

Preheat oven to 350° F. Cream butter and sugar together and add eggs and vanilla. Combine and mix flour, baking powder and baking soda. Add to butter mixture. Fold in sour cream. Spoon half of the batter into a greased and floured bundt pan.

Filling

1/2 cup	almonds, toasted
2 teaspoons	cinnamon
1/2 cup	brown sugar

Combine almonds, cinnamon and brown sugar. Sprinkle on the middle of the batter. Cover the filling with the remaining batter and bake for 35 minutes.

White Chocolate Almond Cakes

8 ounces	almond paste
1/2 cup	sugar
3	eggs
	lemon zest
1/3 cup	all-purpose flour
4 ounces	butter
8 ounces	white chocolate
1 tablespoon	shortening
4 ounces	semisweet chocolate

Preheat oven to 350° F. Beat almond paste with sugar until paste is broken up. Add eggs, one at a time and beat at medium speed until light and fluffy. Near the end of mixing, add the zest. Mix in flour at low speed. Pour batter into a greased and floured cake pan and bake for 18-20 minutes. Remove from oven and cool. Remove cake from pan and cut individual shapes with a moon-shaped cookie cutter.

Meanwhile, place the butter, white chocolate, and shortening in a double boiler and heat until fully combined. Place the cakes on a drying rack and coat with the white chocolate mixture. Melt the semisweet chocolate and drizzle with quick side to side movements over the individual cakes. Allow chocolate to set before serving.

Filo Pastries with Smoked Turkey and Mushrooms

1 cup	mushrooms, minced
2 cloves	garlic, minced
1/4 cup	onion, minced
1/4 cup	sherry
1 teaspoon	olive oil
3 tablespoons	chopped parsley
1/2 cup	crumbled feta cheese
1/4 cup	grated low-fat mozzarella cheese
1/4 teaspoon	dried oregano
1/4 teaspoon	dried thyme
1/4 pound	smoked turkey, minced
15 sheets	filo dough
1/3 cup	unsalted butter, melted

Preheat oven to 350° F. Lightly oil two 9x12-inch baking sheets. In a large skillet over medium high heat, sauté mushrooms, garlic, and onion in sherry and olive oil until soft. Add parsley, feta, mozzarella, oregano, thyme, and turkey. Remove from heat.

Lay filo dough on a clean, dry surface. Cut each sheet in half widthwise to make 30 smaller sheets. Stack them evenly on top of each other, and cover with a piece of plastic wrap and a slightly dampened dish towel as you do the next step.

Butter 1 sheet and cut into 3 long strips. Lay the 3 strips on top of each other. Place about 2 tablespoons of filling in the lower right section near the edge. Fold bottom right corner of filo over filling to meet left edge, creating a small triangle.

Continue folding pastry, as you would a flag, until you reach the top. You will end up with a triangle-shaped pastry.

Lightly butter top of filled triangle and place on prepared baking sheet. Repeat process until all the filling has been used. Bake pastries 20 minutes or until golden. Serve warm.

THE DRAKE HOTEL

Chicago, Illinois

The familiar strains of "As Time Goes By" drift from the harp and across the room as guests sip tea in the low light of Chicago's Palm Court. The setting is only steps away from one of the world's busiest shopping districts, Michigan Avenue's Magnificent Mile. Time does "go by" here - just a little bit slower than the rest of the bustling city. Located in the grand Drake Hotel, business travelers, families on vacation, tired shoppers, and old friends know this as the ideal spot for an afternoon retreat.

Chicagoans often choose this quiet room to commemorate the passing of time. Celebrations regularly unfold here. Young girls enjoying a birthday or couples seated cozily in a quiet corner toasting an anniversary are frequent scenes. This is a place where memories are made.

The classic 13-story hotel with its mammoth rooftop sign has been an icon on Chicago's famous Michigan Avenue since opening in 1921. Built by brothers John and Tracy Drake, the National Registry landmark has hosted numerous world leaders from Emperor Hirohito of Japan to Queen Elizabeth II of England. It recently has been completely restored and is under the management of Hilton International.

Located off the main lobby and up a short wide flight of stairs, the opulent Palm Court is filled with marble-topped tables, cushioned loveseats, and arm chairs set among Chinese lacquered screens and, of course, potted palms. A fantastic crystal chandelier casts a golden light across the room that is reflected in the mirrored columns and ceiling. The harpist is strategically placed at the top of the stairs so that her music lures lobby guests into the palatial setting.

The focal piece of the Palm Court is a fabulous antique urn fountain in the center of the room. Stone cherubs and dolphins frolic around its enormous floral arrangement. The urn looks as if it has always been a part of the Palm Court environment, but, the 270-year old antique was purchased from a New York garden sculpture house only 20 years ago. The room was redesigned around it. The floral print fabrics on the couches, the greenery, the custom built fountain base and lobby appointments were all hand picked to create a proper setting for the baroque urn.

What better way to showcase the elegance of the room than with a proper afternoon tea? The tea choices include standard selections with the interesting addition of an herbal blend called Jet Lag with ginger and peach. The tea is served English style with the tea leaves remaining in the pot.

The three-tiered tray arrives bearing four nicely trimmed tea sandwiches: tomato and cucumber, beef with onion, egg salad, and asparagus rolls. Scones with whipped cream and preserves accompany these. These round yeast scones are more like a bun than a traditional English scone.

Topping off the afternoon is an assortment of pastries including a chocolate torte, lemon squares,

Napoleons, and fresh fruit tarts.

The refreshing respite will undoubtedly renew your energy enough to spend more time exploring the superb cultural opportunities that await you in this museum rich city. The Art Institute of Chicago is a short cab ride south on Michigan Avenue. This is the home of one of the world's best collections of art by Impressionist painters. The Field Museum and Shedd Aquarium are nearby along the shore of Lake Michigan. If your pocketbook allows, you could always spend an hour or two exploring the block-long Marshall Fields store on State Street or taking in one of several theater productions found across the city.

Downtown Chicago is one of the world's easiest big cities to navigate. Its diverse cultural offerings, architectural masterpieces, lakeside vistas and limitless shopping districts make it a city to visit again and again. The Palm Court at the Drake has naturally become a regular stop for returning visitors. It's easy to see why this legendary landmark has established itself as an old friend to so many.

Lemon Squares

1 cup	flour
1/4 cup	confectioners' sugar
1 stick	butter or margarine

Preheat oven to 350° F.

Cut sugar and flour into butter so that it resembles coarse meal. Press firmly into an 8 or 9-inch pan. Bake 15 minutes or until slightly brown.

Topping

2	eggs
1 cup	granulated sugar
1/2 teaspoon	baking powder
2 tablespoons	lemon juice with grated rind

Mix ingredients well and pour over the top of the baked cookie. Bake 20 minutes more at 350° F. Cut into squares while warm and sprinkle thickly with confectioners' sugar.

Currant and Orange Muffins

	safflower oil — to coat muffin tin
1 cup	rice flour
1 tablespoon	baking powder
1 teaspoon	baking soda
1/2 cup	rolled oats, ground
1/4 cup	honey
1 tablespoon	maple syrup
1/4 cup	safflower oil
1/4 cup	ground almonds
1/2 cup	orange juice
1 teaspoon	grated orange rind
2	eggs
1/2 cup	dried currants

Preheat oven to 400° F. Lightly oil a 12-cup muffin pan.

In a large bowl, combine rice flour, baking powder, baking soda, and ground oats.

In a separate bowl combine honey, maple syrup, and the 1/4 cup oil until very smooth. In a blender or food processor, puree almonds and orange juice, then strain. Add almond liquid to honey mixture with orange rind.

Separate eggs. Stir yolks into honey mixture. Beat egg whites until stiff peaks form.

Combine dry and wet ingredients, then stir in currants. Fold in egg whites. Spoon into prepared muffin cups, filling each three fourths full. Bake until muffins spring back when pressed lightly in center (about 20 minutes).

This healthy recipe contains no wheat, refined sugar, or milk.

Egg & Cress Tea Sandwiches

3	medium eggs
2 teaspoons	mayonnaise
dash	salt
dash	pepper
6-8 slices	bread
2 ounces	butter, room temperature
2 bunches	fresh water cress

Boil eggs for 8 minutes. Drain and run under cold water to stop cooking process.

Shell the eggs and mash with a fork until finely chopped. Add mayonnaise, salt, pepper and blend thoroughly.

Spread the bread lightly with butter. Spread the egg mayonnaise generously over half the slices of bread and top with water cress. Press the buttered slices on top. Trim off the crusts and cut into triangles or squares.

DUNBAR TEA ROOM

Sandwich, Massachusettes

No visit to Massachusetts is complete without a visit to Cape Cod. Here lies one of America's great collections of early American villages, homes, shops, lighthouses and pristine beaches. Postcard perfect vistas await you around every turn. Town after town contains white-spire churches and weathered salt box homes. Antique shops spill their wares onto the sidewalks and lovingly restored bed & breakfast inns welcome visitors from around the world. One of the oldest and most picturesque towns on the northern coast is also one of the most accessible.

Founded in 1637, Sandwich became the site of one of America's largest glass factories during the 19th century. The town also was the home of Thornton Burgess, author of *Peter Cottontail.* Here, too, stands the First Church of Christ. Built in 1830, it has a spire designed by noted English architect Christopher Wren. It is one of the most photographed buildings on the cape.

Across the street is the Dexter Grist Mill (dating from the 1640's) where you can see Leo the Miller grinding his corn. Next door is the Thornton Burgess Museum. Just up the street, the Hoxie House, one of the oldest houses on Cape Cod (1675) is furnished with period pieces. Around the corner is Yesteryear's Doll Museum housing an extensive collection of rare and antique dolls.

One of the biggest attractions is the Sandwich Glass Museum and its world class collection of exhibits. The Museum tells the story of a Massachusetts farming community and of Deming Jarves, an entrepreneur from Boston. It is the story of America's decorative glass industry at the dawn of the Industrial Revolution and one of the greatest glass factories, the Boston & Sandwich Glass Company. Fourteen galleries house over 5,000 glass creations on display.

Sandwich also has a number of interesting shops, ranging from a weather store to antique emporia. Visitors often take an afternoon stroll up Grove Street past some grand colonials and the old town burial ground (some grave stones date from the 17th century) to the Heritage Plantation. The 76 acres of beautifully landscaped grounds are home to an antique car museum, a military museum and a working carousel. The famous rhododendrons blossom in May & June.

One of New England's best tea rooms lies in the heart of Sandwich, within the shadow of Christopher Wren's church spire. Since opening in 1991, the Dunbar Tea Room has been featured in many guides, newspapers and magazines from around the world, including *The Boston Globe, The Cape Cod Times, The Washington Post, Yankee Magazine, National Geographic Traveler Magazine, Cape Cod Life, Travel Magazine, Fodor's,* and *Frommer's.*

Tea is served in the former Carriage House, located to the right of the main 1740 house where owners Paula and Jim Hegarty reside. The main

on the buffet. Portions are huge and most customers are seen leaving with a sack of leftovers to enjoy at home.

The Hegartys have found an unbeaten way to make a visit to Cape Cod a deliciously-satisfying experience. Their cozy tea shop has successfully blended the best of old England with the best of New England.

Dundee Squares

2 cups	all-purpose flour
1 cup	sugar
8 ounces	butter
1	large egg, beaten
1 teaspoon	almond extract
12 ounces	semi-sweet chocolate chips
1 cup	raspberry jam
1 cup	slivered almonds

Preheat oven to 350° F. Grease and flour a 9 x 13" pan.

Combine sugar and flour into mixer. Add butter until mixture resembles fine breadcrumbs. Add beaten egg and almond extract until all ingredients are just moistened. Reserve 1 cup of this dough.

Press remaining dough into the bottom of prepared pan. Spread the jam over dough to within 1/2 inch of the edge. Combine reserved cup of dough, chocolate chips, and almonds. Mix well. Sprinkle this mixture over the jam, pressing lightly. Bake 35-40 minutes until golden brown.

Cool slightly, then cut into 12 squares.

dining room sits in an old wood paneled gentlemen's smoking and billiard room.

Now it is home to the clinking of teacups rather than billiard balls, and the air is filled with the aroma of baking pies, cakes, shortbreads and scones rather than pipe smoke. The tea room has a warm fireplace to fight the chill of stiff winter winds. In the summer, customers may sit on the patio or in a shady garden.

The Dunbar Tea Room has become an unique institution and an integral part of a trip to Sandwich. The Hegarty's have developed a great reputation over the years for homemade goods, a wide selection of brewed loose teas and an innovative menu.

Anyone who has traveled to the British Isles will feel right at home with a menu featuring such favorites as a Ploughman's Lunch, Smoked Scottish Salmon Platter, English crumpets, petticoat shortbread and, of course, scones with jam and cream. Tea is made British style - loose tea in the pot with a silver strainer. Cozies keep the tea piping hot.

Guests need to pace themselves so that they save room for a slice of one of the cakes or pies displayed

Queen Mother's Cake

8 ounces	chopped, pitted dates
1 cup	boiling water
1 teaspoon	baking soda
3 ounces	butter
1 cup	sugar
1	egg, beaten
1 teaspoon	vanilla
1 teaspoon	salt
1 teaspoon	baking powder
1 1/4 cups	flour
2 ounces	chopped walnuts

Preheat oven to 350° F. Grease and flour an 8-inch square cake pan.

Pour the boiling water over the chopped dates, add baking soda and set aside. Beat the butter and sugar together until light and fluffy, add egg, and vanilla. Mix in salt, baking powder, and flour until well blended. Add walnuts and date mixture, mix for 1-2 minutes longer. Bake for 50-60 minutes. Cool completely.

Topping

5 tablespoons	brown sugar
2 tablespoons	butter
2 tablespoons	heavy cream
	chopped walnuts

In a medium saucepan, mix topping ingredients together. Bring to a boil. Simmer for 3 minutes only, stirring occasionally. Pour over cake and sprinkle with chopped walnuts.

The Dunbar

Base

1 3/4 cup	all-purpose flour
1/3 cup	sugar
6 ounces	butter

Preheat oven to 350° F.

For the base, mix together flour, sugar and butter until well blended. Press mixture evenly into a 7 x 11-inch baking pan. Bake 15 minutes or light brown.

Filling

1 can	condensed milk
8 ounces	butter
4 tablespoons	golden syrup
1 cup	sugar

Place all filling ingredients in medium saucepan and bring to a boil. Simmer stirring constantly for 5-8 minutes. The mixture will thicken and turn a light brown color. Pour the mixture over the cooked base and allow to cool completely.

Glaze

| 2 ounces | milk chocolate, melted |

Melt the chocolate and spread evenly over the top. Cool before cutting into slices.

Apricot Bars

2/3 cup	dried apricots
1 stick	unsalted butter, softened
1/4 cup	granulated sugar
1 1/3 cups	all-purpose flour
1 cup	packed light brown sugar
2	large eggs
1/2 cup	chopped walnuts
1/2 teaspoon	baking powder
1/2 teaspoon	salt
	confectioners' sugar for dusting

Preheat oven to 350° F.

In a small saucepan, simmer apricots in water, covered, for 15 minutes. Drain, then cool to room temperature. Chop finely. Beat together butter, granulated sugar, and 1 cup flour with an electric mixer, on medium speed, until mixture resembles coarse crumbs. Press evenly over bottom of a greased 8-inch square metal baking pan (not non-stick) and bake in the middle of the oven until golden, about 25 minutes.

Beat together chopped apricots, brown sugar, eggs, walnuts, baking powder, vanilla, salt and remaining 1/3 cup flour on medium speed until combined well. Pour topping over crust and bake in middle of oven until topping is set and golden, 25 to 30 minutes more.

Cool in pan on a rack and cut into 12 bars. Dust with confectioners' sugar.

Preheat oven to 400° F.

Saute onion and garlic in small amount of oil. Remove from heat and add herbs.

Mix together cream cheese, mustard, crab, flour, and onion mixture until well blended. Add salt and pepper to taste.

Place 1 sheet of puff pastry into a greased 10" tart pan. Add crab mixture. Place puff pastry sheet on top. Crimp together with a fork. Brush with beaten egg and sprinkle with some mixed herbs and dill. Cut a few slits into the top of the puff pastry. Bake in oven at 400° F for 20-25 minutes until well risen and golden brown.

Deviled Crab Tart

2 sheets	puff pastry
2 cloves	garlic, crushed
1 pound	cream cheese softened
4 tablespoons	mustard
1 pound	fresh crab meat
1	egg, beaten
1	onion chopped
2 tablespoons	mixed herbs
1/2 cup	flour
3 tablespoons	fresh chopped dill
	salt and pepper

DUSHANBE TEAHOUSE

Boulder, Colorado

Taking tea with friends has been a unifying experience for centuries. No where is the convivial custom more evident than in the Rocky Mountains north of Denver. The sister cities of Boulder, Colorado and Dushanbe, Tajikistan have taken the art and camaraderie of tea to its highest level.

In 1987, during his first visit to Boulder, Dushanbe's Mayor Maksud Ikramov announced that he planned to present the city with a teahouse to celebrate the establishment of sister city ties. Dushanbe {doo-shan-bay'} is the capital of Tajikistan. The name, meaning "Monday," is derived from the day of the week on which a bazaar was held in the village on the site.

Using skills handed down from generation to generation, more than 40 artisans in several cities of Tajikistan created the decorative elements for the teahouse, including its hand-carved and hand-painted ceiling, tables, stools, columns, and ceramic panels.

In Central Asia, teahouses serve as gathering places where friends meet to talk or play chess over a cup of tea. Many teahouses are traditionally decorated with lavish Persian art, characterized by the use of motifs from nature - stellar, solar, and floral. The Dushanbe Teahouse accurately reflects this artistic tradition dating back nearly 2,000 years. The master woodcarvers who helped reassemble the teahouse here have carved their names in the ceiling. The artisans who painted it have written their names on a green painted area above the entry to the kitchen. A message carved into the ceiling reads "artisans of ancient Khojand whose works are magical."

A magical place it is! The aroma of curry and other exotic spices greets guests as they enter. One corner has a low table surrounded by pillows where guests are invited to recline for their tea - as in a Bedouin tent. The center of the room is dominated by a central pool surrounded by seven hammered copper sculptures created by artist Ivan Milosovich. The life sized feminine images are based on a 12th century poem, "The Seven Beauties."

The ceiling of the Teahouse was carved and painted with intricate traditional Persian art patterns. The ceiling was originally built, carved and painted in Tajikistan. Absolutely no power tools were used in the original construction. The work was crafted by hand, exactly as it was centuries ago. Inside the teahouse, there are 12 intricately carved cedar columns. No two columns are alike.

Eight colorful ceramic panels, created by Victor Zabolotnikov, grace the building's exterior and display patterns of a "Tree of Life." Each panel was sculpted in Tajikistan, cut into smaller tiles, fired, and then carefully packed to be sent to Boulder. Once here, they were repositioned by the artist.

The Teahouse offers an eclectic mix of dishes from around the world with an emphasis on traditional Tajik and Persian entrees such as Lamb

Shish Kabob and Persian Vegetarian Kooftah Balls.

A more traditional afternoon tea is served on white linen with an assortment of pastries and sweets, scones with cream and lemon curd, tea sandwiches, and a choice of brewed teas served in Chatsford pots. Reservations are required 24 hours in advance for this tea time in Boulder's most exotic atmosphere.

Anyone who appreciates tea will want to visit the nearby Celestial Seasonings factory, appropriately located at the edge of town on Sleepy Time Lane. The free hour-long tour begins in a sampling room where guests sample hot or cold teas and then record their tea reviews. An informative video gives everyone a history of the colorful Boulder industry that now produces over a million tea bags each day. The leisurely tour through the working area of the plant is highlighted by stepping into the eye-opening peppermint vault and a fascinating view of the blending and packaging areas.

These two tea experiences in Boulder are unlike anything you will find in America. A trip to this college town at the base of the Rocky Mountains gives you new insight into the wide world of tea.

Banana Fritters

4	ripe bananas, mashed
3/4 cup	all-purpose flour
2	eggs, beaten
3 tablespoons	sugar
	vegetable oil
	cinnamon sugar

In a bowl, combine first 4 ingredients. Mix thoroughly and beat slightly.

Drop 1 full tablespoon of this mixture onto a hot, greased griddle. Fry on both sides.

Serve with cinnamon sugar.

Curry-Cheese Biscuits

2 cups	all-purpose flour, sifted
1/2 teaspoon	salt
1/2 teaspoon	dry mustard
1 1/2 teaspoons	curry powder
1/16 teaspoon	cayenne pepper
2/3 cup	butter or margarine
1 cup	sharp cheddar cheese, grated
1	egg, beaten
2 tablespoons	milk

Preheat oven to 400° F.

Combine the first 5 ingredients in a mixing bowl. Add butter and cut it into fine crumb consistency.

Add the cheese. Stir in beaten egg and milk.

Turn out onto a pastry board while still in the crumbly stage. Form into a mound with hands. Cut through the center of mound with a spatula. Stack half of the crumbly mound on the other half and again shape into a mound. Repeat this process until the dough holds together, about 10-12 times.

Roll into 1/16-inch thickness. Cut with a 2-inch cookie cutter. Bake for 10 minutes.

Teahouse Gingerbread

3 1/2 cups	all-purpose flour
2 teaspoons	baking powder
2/3 teaspoon	powdered ginger
2/3 teaspoon	cinnamon
1 1/3 cups	canola oil
3	medium eggs
1/3 cup	honey
1/3 cup	molasses
1/3 cup	sugar
1 1/3 cup	brewed Boulder Tangerine Herbal Infusion, available from Teahouse

Preheat oven to 400° F.

In a large bowl, mix oil, eggs, honey, molasses, and sugar. Beat at medium speed, scraping often, until creamy. Reduce to low speed and add tea. Mix well.

Add sifted dry ingredients. Mix until moistened.

Pour into 2 oiled and floured 9x13" baking pans. Bake 35-40 minutes or until set.

Chutney Crescents

1/2 cup	butter or margarine
3 ounces	cream cheese
1 cup	all-purpose flour, sifted
1/2 cup	chutney
1/3 cup	sugar
1 teaspoon	ground cinnamon

Cream butter and cream cheese until smoothly blended. Beat in flour.

Shape dough into smooth ball, wrap in waxed paper, and chill overnight.

Remove dough from refrigerator 30 minutes before using.

Preheat oven to 400° F.

Roll dough to1/3-inch thickness and cut with a 3-inch cookie cutter. Place small spoonful of chutney in center of each round. Fold over; press edges together.

Bake on ungreased baking sheet for 15 minutes. Roll in sugar mixed with cinnamon.

QUEEN MARY TEA ROOM

Seattle, Washington

Seattle is a town that sees a lot of overcast days. Dark gray clouds, laden with warm Pacific moisture, blow in regularly from the west and drop their burdens on the rich green landscape. Generous rain is great for the profuse flora that thrives in this moisture-rich environment, but the lack of sunshine can take its toll on the inhabitants of this sun-deprived corner of Washington. Residents long for a reprieve from the overcast skies and a comforting dose of hot tea to carry them over to the next ray of sunshine.

Since 1988, the tea drinking populace of Seattle has turned to an ivy-covered, English-style tea room for a bit of solace and a generous helping of British comfort food. Each customer of The Queen Mary Tea Room is given a royal welcome by the owner Mary Greengo.

Mary has always had a reputation for looking after details. One envious friend once commented, "Who do you think you are? Queen Mary?" The name was too good to let go, and Mary claimed the moniker as the name for her storefront restaurant that sits along an incline 10 blocks north of the University of Washington.

Brightly waving banners and overflowing flower boxes beckon guests as they approach the door. To the left of the front door, Mary's caged birds sing to all who pass by. The front door opens to a shop filled with tea gifts and accoutrements. Glittering delights are stacked to the ceiling in an overwhelming display of tea temptations. This is an Anglophile's dream. There is even a pastry case as you enter, stocked with tea cakes, trifle, and Devon double cream so that you can go home and recreate your tea experience all over again.

You would have to travel to Somerset to find a more genuine Jane Austen eatery. Laura Ashley chintz and lace abound. The wood-panel wainscoted walls are brightened by gilded mirrors and an endless collection of brightly-colored tea wares lining the room. Floral curtains, wicker chairs and puffy pillows give the feel of an English cottage.

The décor is just the beginning of your state-side journey into British cuisine. The menu is filled with tea room classics such as Shepherd's Pie, Cornish Beef Pasties, crumpets, and scones with cream and strawberry jam.

The real jewel in the crown of this royal retreat is a tea list that would be hard to find in a tea room in England. Over 50 teas fill the extensive inventory that boasts beautiful white, green, oolong and black teas, as well as herbal tisanes and flavored teas from around the world. Why drink a common Earl Grey or English Breakfast when you can choose a Golden Pu-erh or a rare White Darjeeling? Each pot is made fresh and brought piping hot to the table in a press pot. Queen Mary puts the "tea" in tea room!

Afternoon tea can be as simple as a pot of tea with a Queen Mum Cookie, or a Royal Afternoon

Tea featuring course after course of traditional savories and sweets complimented with a flute of sparkling wine. The crustless tea sandwiches, pastries and cakes are all made in-house by Mary and her talented staff. Many of the recipes have been handed down through the owner's family for generations.

The royal theme often carries over to the customers. Don't be surprised to see a few diners wearing tiaras. Ladies at tea like to feel a bit regal sometimes.

"It's amazing how your day can change once you don a tiara," Mary likes to say. The Queen-in-residence will lend you a faux-diamond diadem should you forget to bring your own. It's just another of the countless details that she pays attention to daily.

Warm Chocolate Pudding Cakes

12 ounces	bittersweet chocolate
1 cup	butter

Place chocolate and butter into a small saucepan. Warm over low heat until melted. Set aside.

Prepare 6 ramekins by lightly buttering the interiors. Preheat oven to 350° F.

1 cup	sugar
1/2 cup	all-purpose flour
6	eggs

Combine sugar and flour in a large mixing bowl. Add eggs, one at a time, and beat together until fluffy, about 5 minutes. Add chocolate until mixed thoroughly.

Pour into 6 prepared ramekins. Bake for 15 minutes. Serve warm.

Thumbprint Cookies

4 ounces	butter, softened
1 cup	shortening
1 cup	brown sugar
2 1/2 teaspoons	vanilla
4	egg yolks
4 cups	all-purpose flour
3/4 teaspoon	salt
4	egg whites, beaten
1/4 cup	hazelnuts, chopped fine
1 small jar	raspberry or apricot preserves

Preheat oven to 350° F. Cream together butter, shortening, brown sugar, and vanilla. Add yolks, one at a time. Add flour and salt. Mix until just combined.

Place scoops of dough onto a baking sheet, then flatten. Coat top with egg whites and lightly sprinkle with hazelnuts. Bake 15 minutes or until firm.

Remove from oven and make a thumbprint in the center of each cookie while still warm. Fill with preserves. Allow to cool before serving.

Lemon Meringues

3	egg whites
1/2 teaspoon	cream of tartar
1 cup	sugar
Pinch	salt
1/2 teaspoon	vanilla

Place egg whites in a mixing bowl. Using a whisk attachment, add cream of tartar and beat on high speed. Mix until frothy. Add sugar and salt a little at a time. Add vanilla. Continue to whip until stiff peaks form.

Preheat oven to 200° F. Line a baking sheet with parchment paper. Spoon or pipe a "bird's nest" of meringue, 1-2 inches in circumference.

Place in oven for 1 hour (check to make sure they do not brown).

Turn oven off and leave an additional two hours or overnight.

When dry and cool, fill with lemon curd.

Mint Butter

2 cups	sweet butter, softened
1 cup	mint leaves, rinsed
1 teaspoon	lemon juice
1 teaspoon	salt
1 teaspoon	sugar

Using a food processor, make a purée of all ingredients. Rub through a fine sieve if desired. Spoon into plastic containers and chill until needed. (May be frozen.)

Allow butter to come to room temperature before using. Serve with warm scones or spread over a toasted English muffin.

Victorian Sponge

4 ounces	butter, room temperature
1/2 cup	granulated sugar
2	medium eggs, beaten
1 cup	self-rising flour
1 tablespoon	boiling water
1/3 cup	raspberry jam
1 tablespoon	confectioners' sugar

Preheat oven to 350° F.

Grease and line two 7-inch round cake pans.

With an electric mixer, cream butter and sugar together until light and fluffy. Beat in eggs, a little at a time, alternating with 1 tablespoon of flour between each addition. Beat thoroughly.

Fold in remaining flour with a metal spoon. Stir in the boiling water and mix well.

Divide the mixture between the prepared pans and bake for 20-25 minutes or until the cake is lightly browned and springs back when pressed lightly with your finger. Remove from the oven and place on a wire rack to cool.

When cold, spread the underside of one cake with jam. Lay the other cake carefully on top. Cover lightly with sifted confectioners' sugar.

Although raspberry jam is the most common filling for a classic Victorian Sponge, lemon or raspberry curd also makes a delicious filling between the layered cakes.

Lemon Curd

3	eggs
1/2 cup	fresh lemon juice
1/2 cup	unsalted butter, melted
1 cup	sugar

In the top part of a double boiler, beat eggs until frothy. Stir in lemon juice, sugar and melted butter. Place over simmering water. Stir constantly for 20 minutes. The mixture should become slightly thickened.

Remove from heat and spoon into a pint-sized container. Cool to room temperature, cover and refrigerate for at least two hours before serving. Keeps well for two weeks.

THE FAIRMONT EMPRESS HOTEL

Victoria, British Columbia

There is a bit of Britain nestled beside a rugged bay on an enchanted island in the southwest corner of British Columbia, where the gentle custom of afternoon tea is still celebrated in grand style. "More English than the English" was true of the first English-born Victorians who established Fort Victoria in 1843, seeking to create a society based on a nostalgic, half-remembered homeland. Today the city of Victoria has grown into one of the top 10 urban destinations for world travelers. At the city's heart, welcoming guests as they arrive by boat or ferry, is the magnificent Fairmont Empress Hotel.

Since its opening in 1908, the hotel has long been accustomed to entertaining Hollywood celebrities. Rita Hayworth, Jack Benny, Bob Hope, Bing Crosby, Tallulah Bankhead, Barbara Streisand, Harrison Ford and a host of others have passed through its lobby. Shirley Temple arrived accompanied by her parents amid rumors that she had fled from California because of kidnapping threats, a story born from the presence of two huge bodyguards who took the room opposite hers and always left their door open.

By 1965, there was much debate on whether to tear down what was becoming a faded, dowdy hotel, to make room for a more modern, functional high-rise hotel. One local newspaper warned that, "Without this splendid relic of the Edwardian era, literally tens of thousands of tourists will never return. This is the Mecca, this is the heart and soul of the city." The decision was announced on June 10, 1966: The Fairmont Empress would not be demolished. Instead she would embark on a $4 million campaign of renovation and refurbishment, playfully dubbed "Operation Teacup."

Stories of unusual guests and employees abound. In 1987, a woman wrote about her wonderful stay at The Fairmont Empress and asked if other guests had received a similar late night visitor - a little girl who had watched over her bed and then floated across the room. There also are the stories of an early 20th century maid, who appears now and then on the sixth floor to help with the cleaning.

In 1989, over $45 million was spent on the royal restoration. All guest rooms were renovated, and a health club, indoor swimming pool and guest reception were added. With an emphasis on craftsmanship, no attempt was made to give the hotel a new image. Instead, the goal was to restore The Fairmont Empress to her original elegance.

The strong emotion The Fairmont Empress evokes is exemplified in the statement made by an irate gentleman, as workers raised the sign above the front entrance, "Anyone who doesn't know this is The Empress shouldn't be staying here."

Afternoon tea is *what you do* when you visit Victoria, and nowhere is this daily celebration observed more royally than in the opulent Fairmont Empress Hotel. In all of North America, there is not a tea venue which has introduced more guests to the pleasures of afternoon tea.

Guests are invited to sip tea and enjoy delicious food and pleasant conversation accompanied by relaxing music, while seated in the famous Tea Lobby. The rose and green-trimmed lobby ceiling is over 15 feet high and supports 12 original chandeliers. A pair of period portraits of George V and Queen Mary stand watch over the matching fireplaces. Tea patrons are seated at comfortable couches or chintz-covered high-back chairs set before antique wooden tea tables.

Summertime guests may take their tea at wicker tables along the verandah and watch boats arriving in the harbor, as travelers have done for a century.

In cooler months, a leisurely tea at the Empress begins with Fresh fruit with chantilly cream is offered in season. The signature tea is a blend of China, Darjeeling, and Ceylon teas, called *The Empress Blend*. Each guest receives a gift box as a souvenir.

The highlight of the meal is the arrival of a three-tiered china rack laden with traditional tea sandwiches-smoked salmon, deviled egg, sliced cucumber-and raisin scones, accompanied by Jersey cream and strawberry preserves.

Delicious shortbread crescents, light chocolate tortes, and sweet strawberry tarts fill out the top tier. Fortunately you may have as many as you wish!

A great way to walk off those clotted cream calories is to wander through the variety of fascinating shops that line nearby Government Street. One of the most interesting is Murchies', an outstanding tea shop and bakery. This is no ordinary tea store. This is one of the largest retail outlets in the world for tea, teapots, books and every known tea accoutrement. Tea devotees will spend hours, and many Canadian dollars, here.

The Fairmont Empress is not content to rest on its laurels. In a world where tea drinkers are becoming more and more sophisticated, this jewel in the Fairmont Hotels and Resorts crown has a reputation to maintain. Luckily for visitors to this paradise, the celebration of afternoon tea has been, and will continue to be, one of the unforgettable memories delighted visitors carry back to the real world.

Fairmont Empress Lemon Tarts

1 cup	lemon juice
	zest of 1 lemon
1 1/2 cups	sugar
6	eggs
1 2/3 cups	double cream
8	pre-baked tart shells

Preheat oven to 300°F.

Combine lemon juice, zest, and sugar. Whisk in eggs and cream.

Spoon mixture into pre-baked tart shells. Bake for 25 minutes. Sprinkle with granulated sugar and place under a broiler until caramelized.

Serve with a dollop of whipped cream.

Sour Cherry Bakewell Slices

1 1/4 cups	butter
1 1/4 cups	sugar
2 cups	almond paste
9	eggs
1/4 cup	all-purpose flour
1 teaspoon	baking powder
3/4 cup	canned sour cherries (drained)
1/4 cup	sliced almonds

Preheat oven to 325°F.

Grease and line a round cake pan. Combine butter, sugar, and almond paste. Cream until smooth. Slowly add the eggs. Fold in flour and baking powder. Add sour cherries and mix.

Pour into prepared pan and sprinkle with almonds. Bake for 45 minutes. Allow to cool before slicing.

Fairmont Empress Scones

3 cups	all-purpose flour
1/2 cup	sugar
1 cup	butter
2 tablespoons	baking powder
2	eggs
1 cup	cream
1 cup	golden raisins
	egg wash

Preheat oven to 325°F.

Mix the flour, butter, sugar, and baking powder together. In a separate bowl, mix cream and eggs together. Add raisins to flour mixture. Gradually add liquid to the dry mixture. Do not over mix.

Roll out to the thickness of 1 inch. Allow the dough to rest.

Cut with 2 1/2" cutter. Let rest for 3/4 hour. Brush tops with an eggwash and bake for 20-25 minutes or until golden brown.

THE FARMHOUSE TEA SHOPPE

Dunwoody, Georgia

The once-quiet rural town of Dunwoody, Georgia has changed dramatically through the past 30 years. General stores and simple farm homes once lined the dusty, clay-covered country roads that meandered through pine groves and across countless cotton fields. These pastoral scenes have long been swallowed by the encroaching metropolis of Atlanta. Suburban life and all its "busy-ness" has taken over. It is in the midst of the bumper-to-bumper commuter traffic and endless shopping malls that we find one of the last vestiges of Dunwoody's former self.

The Farmhouse Tea Shoppe sits on an oasis of green lawn and pecan trees in the heart of Dunwoody. In fact, the building's restorers, the Dunwoody Preservation Trust, had a vision that this 1906 National Historical Registry home should be the literal and figurative "heart" of the community.

Built by cotton farmer Joberry Creek, the Upper Piedmont Plain Style home now serves as both a home to the Farmhouse Tea Shoppe and a gallery for the Dunwoody Arts Association. Climbing the steps to the rambling front porch with its enticing wooden rockers reminds many guests of visiting their grandparents' houses.

Upon entering, guests immediately notice the detailed planning that went into bringing this architectural gem back to life: soothing pale yellow walls, custom window treatments, and restored wooden floors. Framed watercolors, pastels, oil paintings and photographs, all for sale, fill the walls. Around a corner in a side room, are the tea goodies - a gift shop brimming with fragrant teas, pots, books, cozies, and precious accoutrements.

Lunch and tea are served in four rooms, each containing a variety of antique tables covered with pastel linens, bowls of brown and white sugar crystals, and topped with impressive soaring glass flower stands. Even the butter pats are molded in the shapes of daisies and roses. Folded wooden muffineers sit beside the fireplace waiting placement beside the tables where they will hold an array of cozy-covered teapots. The carefully selected offering of loose teas includes many traditional blends, as well as a nice selection of Darjeelings, green teas, and South African rooibos.

This authentic tea setting, where every detail is well-planned, was origanlly designed by Val Shave and Lana Quibell. These gracious ladies with South African roots carried out their dream of bringing a genuine "old world" afternoon tea experience to the Atlanta area. New owner Debbie Seven is keeping that dream alive.

Tea room in the South conjures up images of plain chicken salad scooped onto a lettuce leaf, and accompanied by a glass of sweet ice tea. The Farmhouse has taken this chicken dish to new heights.

Diners can't help but notice plate after plate of the wildly popular Oriental chicken salad coming out of the kitchen. This is a mound of seasoned chopped chicken breast, laced with toasted almonds and noodles with shredded Napa cabbage. More colorful and slightly less textural is a sister dish, lightly curried chicken salad enhanced with a curry mayonnaise. Also included on the menu is a flaky, pastry-wrapped mélange of curried lamb, raisins, almonds and fruit chutney called *Bobotie* in South Africa. The carrot bisque is nothing short of heaven, creamy but not cloying, the refreshing sweetness of the carrot balanced by the crunchy tang of shredded caramelized onion. These luncheon items are spectacular but they pale in comparison to the afternoon tea celebration.

The Windsor Afternoon Tea begins with a selection of traditional tea sandwiches and savories. The crusts are all neatly trimmed and every creation is presented in beautiful fashion. The menu changes regularly as the owners discover new regional and international items. They even have included an English savory rarely found this side of London, homemade sausage rolls — not spicy, just savory. These flaky rolls of baked pastry are filled with just the right amount of seasoned meat.

The savories are followed by a satisfying selection of sweets and sultana scones with preserves and, of course, Devonshire cream. These are true scones, not triangle-shaped clumps of dough sold under the same name in bakeries and coffee shops around town. Guests may take frozen ones home to re-create their own tea experience.

No afternoon tea is complete without a cake course. The problem here is deciding whether to choose the homemade layer cakes or the signature Passion Fruit Roulade. You may be lucky enough to spot a pastry swan covered in powdered sugar or one of the other assorted pastries of the day.

Adults may choose to begin their tea celebration with a glass of champagne. For the children, there is a Mad Hatter's Tea featuring hot chocolate or fruit infusions, along with sandwiches and sweets with young appetites in mind.

The town of Dunwoody is fortunate to have this exquisite tea room at its heart. Many residents realize that tea has helped preserve a bit of their local history. The Farmhouse ladies help them remember the slower pace of the past as they race toward the future.

Praline Pecan Kisses

1 cup	light brown sugar
1	egg white, beaten stiff
1 1/2 cups	pecan halves

Preheat oven to 250° F. Line a cookie sheet with aluminum foil.

Beat egg white until stiff peaks form. Gradually add sugar. Fold in pecans. Drop teaspoon mounds on aluminum foil. Bake 30-35 minutes. Allow to cool. Remove from foil.

Passion Fruit Roulade

1 1/2 cups	sugar
1 cup	all-purpose flour
1 teaspoon	baking powder
1 teaspoon	baking soda
1/2 teaspoon	salt
6	large egg yolks
1/2 cup	vegetable oil
1/2 cup	water
2 tablespoons	vanilla
6	large egg whites

Preheat oven to 350°F. Spray a 1/2" sheet pan with cooking spray, line with parchment paper and spray again lightly.

Sift together 1 cup sugar, flour, soda, and baking powder. Add salt. In a bowl, combine the yolks, oil, water, and vanilla. Gradually add dry ingredients. Set aside.

Beat 6 egg whites and add remaining 1/2 cup sugar. Fold about 1/3 whites into dough mixture to lighten. Gradually add remaining whites. Pour into prepared pan and bake 10-12 minutes. Cool on a rack.

Filling

1 1/2 cups	whipping cream
1/3 cup	confectioners sugar, sifted
1 1/2 teaspoon	unflavored gelatin
4 tablespoons	cold water
1/4 cup	passion fruit concentrate (frozen fruit juice reduced 1/2 by boiling)

Dissolve gelatin in cold water and allow to bloom. Place over hot water until melted. Allow to cool just until tepid, but not cool.

Beat cream until foamy. Slowly add the confectioners sugar and whip to soft peaks. Add cool gelatin and passion fruit. Continue to whip until fairly stiff.

Spread towel on counter and sprinkle with sifted confectioners sugar. Turn cake on a towel and remove paper. Spread filling onto cake, leaving about 1 inch on one long edge. Roll cake and filling, using towel to assist with rolling, moving towards the uncoated edge. Place on tray and refrigerate.

Frosting

4 cups	confectioners' sugar, sifted
1/4 cup	passion fruit concentrate
2 tablespoons	heavy cream

Combine 3 1/2 cups sugar with passion fruit and cream. Add sugar as needed. Spread on cake.

Cream Puff Swans

1 cup	water
4 tablespoons	unsalted butter
dash	salt
1 cup	flour
4	eggs

Preheat oven to 370° F. Bring water, butter, and salt to a boil in a saucepan. After the butter has melted, add the flour. Mix quickly with a wooden spoon until batter is smooth. Continue to stir for a few minutes over low heat in order to dry the dough. The dough should not stick to your fingers when touched. Transfer the dough to a clean bowl and let it cool. Beat while adding eggs, one at a time, until mixture is smooth. Grease and flour a cookie sheet. Using about 3/4 of the dough, drop large tablespoons of dough (2" diameter) onto the prepared sheet.

Place the remaining batter into a pastry tube fitted with a large round tip. Pipe the batter onto a prepared baking sheet in the shape of an "S". Brush all the shapes with beaten egg and let dry for 25 minutes.

Bake for 30-35 minutes or until light brown. Turn off heat, open the oven door slightly, and let the puffs cool in the oven for 20 minutes. Cool completely.

Filling

2 cups	heavy cream
1/2 cup	sugar
1 tablespoon	vanilla

Whip the heavy cream until slightly thickened. Add sugar and continue whipping until the cream is thick. Fold in the vanilla. Split the puffs in half horizontally. Then split the top in half to make wings. Fill the bottom half with cream. Place an "S" in the cream for a neck and head. Add the wings. Refrigerate until ready to serve.

Oriental Chicken Salad

1 head	Napa cabbage
2	green lettuce leaves
1	carrot, coarsely grated
4-5 cups	cooked chicken breast, diced

Slice cabbage and lettuce finely. Combine with carrot and diced chicken.

1 package	Ramen noodles (discard the flavor packet)
20 ounces	slivered almonds
1/4 cup	sesame seeds
1/3 stick	butter

Crush the noodles well in unopened bag. Melt the butter in a skillet over medium heat. Fry the noodles, almonds, and sesame seeds until golden brown. Stir constantly to avoid burning.

Dressing

1 packet	Good Seasonings Oriental Sesame Dressing
2 tablespoons	sugar

Make dressing according to package directions. Add sugar.

Put all ingredients together and just before serving, toss generously with dressing to taste.

"If you are cold, tea will warm you; if you are depressed, it will cheer you; if you are excited, it will calm you."
William Gladstone

DISNEY'S GRAND FLORIDIAN RESORT & SPA

Walt Disney World Resort
Lake Buena Vista, Florida

It is no surprise that the people who specialize in making magical kingdoms also know how to create a beautiful afternoon tea. Guests at Walt Disney's Grand Floridian Resort & Spa quickly realize the Garden View Tea Room is the perfect spot for relaxing during a busy Disney vacation. This civilized haven offers solitude and refined service for weary adults who have explored Epcot, the Magic Kingdom Park, Disney's Animal Kingdom and Disney-MGM Studios to the point of fatigue. There are no lines here, no children tugging at your sleeve, no weather worries. The biggest decision you make all afternoon is what kind of tea you will have.

Disney's Grand Floridian Resort & Spa has the feel of a magnificent Victorian hotel on a tropical island. The resort opened in July 1988 and is considered the flagship of all Disney resorts. The 867-room facility located on the shores of Seven Seas Lagoon is southwest, and one monorail stop, from the Magic Kingdom Park. The great white wooden main building features a spectacular red gabled roof and a five-story Grand Lobby.

Guests stepping into the Grand Lobby are swept back into Queen Victoria's day: spacious verandahs, crystal chandeliers, stained-glass ceiling, exotic aviary, and nine-foot ebony grand piano. An impressive staircase leads to the second floor where comfortable sitting areas await guests with tired feet.

The Tea Room sits at the end of the Grand Lobby.

The coral walls, white woodwork, and splendid gold mirrors all add to the gentle calm of the island motif. An entire wall of tall arched windows let in the bright Florida sunshine and give an unobstructed view of the floral gardens, pools, and beaches that fill the grounds. It's not uncommon to see brides in wedding dresses trailed by ladies in waiting and family photographers walking through the outdoor gardens. The popular Fairy Tale Wedding Pavilion sits on a private island in the lagoon.

The Tea Room is filled with a variety of marble-topped tables and comfortable upholstered arm chairs. Each table is set with Royal Doulton China. An impressive floral display crowns a draped round double-tiered table filled with trays of delicious pastries, bowls of strawberries and cream, and a colorful English trifle. White wooden trolleys are topped with rows of teapots waiting to be filled with piping hot water and fine loose teas.

A variety of tea meals are offered in the Tea Room. The Grand Tea is a classic traditional English afternoon menu offering a variety of tea sandwiches, scones, tarts, pastries, English trifle, tea and champagne. The sandwich selections are always changing but they often include egg & chive, salmon spread, watercress and cucumber, and chicken with almonds.

The Buckingham Palace service includes sandwiches, scones, jam tarts, strawberries with cream and tea. The lighter Sally Lunn Tea is similar to a quick English Cream Tea featuring Sally Lunn Rolls with apricot preserves, strawberries and cream, and a pot of tea. A children's tea with mouseketeer-friendly sandwiches and hot chocolate also is offered.

One unique menu choice is the Prince Edward's Gentlemen's Tea. This savory offering seems intent on coaxing novice male tea drinkers into a venue often dominated by women. Chef Cheryl Smith has put together a fantastic presentation of duck liver en croute, country pâté, potted crab crostini and marinated fresh berries, all served with a delicious Cumberland sauce. Scones with Devonshire cream accompany the feast along with a pot of tea and a glass of port. Close your eyes while eating and you can imagine yourself in a fine country house hotel in England's Lake District.

The Grand Floridian atmosphere is elegant, but in a friendly Disney way. Guests are made to feel special and appreciated. They often leave refreshed and inspired. The Grand Floridian transports you to a magical place and leaves you with a lasting memory. Isn't that what tea has been doing for centuries?

Chicken and Almond Tea Sandwich

8 ounces	chicken white meat, cooked and ground
4 ounces	slivered almonds, lightly toasted
4 ounces	heavy cream to bind
dash	salt
dash	fresh cracked black pepper

In a bowl, fold all ingredients.

Basil Butter

16 ounces	unsalted butter
1 tablespoon	tomato puree
1 teaspoon	lemon juice
1/2 teaspoon	sugar
1/2 teaspoon	salt
4 ounces	chiffonade of basil

Puree first 5 ingredients. Fold in basil.

Lightly spread softened basil butter on thin slices of marble rye bread. Add light amount of chicken paste to half the slices. Top with buttered bread. Trim edges and cut into triangles.

Sally Lunns

1 cup	milk
1/4 cup	sugar
2 teaspoons	salt
1 stick	butter
1/2 cup	very warm water
1 package	dry yeast
3	eggs
4 1/2 cups	all-purpose flour

In a pan, scald the milk. Add sugar, salt, and butter. Cool to lukewarm.

In a large bowl, dissolve yeast in the warm water. Add lukewarm milk mixture, eggs, and flour. Beat until smooth. Cover and allow to rise for 1 hour.

Preheat oven to 350° F. Stir dough again and pour into a large, prepared loaf pan. Let rise for 30 minutes in a warm, draft-free area.

Bake for 40 minutes or until crusty and brown. Remove from pan to rack. Brush with butter. Serve warm or toasted with butter and preserves.

Potted Crab Crostini

2 pounds	jumbo lump crab
1	orange
4 ounces	dry sherry
4 ounces	unsalted butter
1/2 teaspoon	salt
1/2 teaspoon	fresh ground black pepper
3 drops	Tabasco
	baguette crostini
1/2 cup	clarified butter (optional)

Zest and juice the orange. In a small sauce pan, place orange zest, orange juice, and sherry. Simmer and reduce by half. Strain mixture through a cheese cloth. In a food processor, beat butter and orange reduction until smooth, then add crab. Continue to blend as you add salt, pepper, and Tabasco.

When smooth, remove to a piping bag with a #10 tip. Slice baguettes into 1/4-inch thick diagonal slices. Spray with clarified butter (or baking spray) and toast on a sheet pan in a hot oven until brown.

Pipe potted crab on crostini and drizze with a tiny bit of clarified butter.

MISS MABLE'S

Dickson, Tennessee

Open the door to any successful tea room and you're likely to find an owner with great passion and an unending desire to offer warm hospitality and outstanding service. Miss Mables's Tea Room in Dickson, Tennessee, is a shining example of why Americans are returning to tea rooms and tea shops in growing numbers.

Who's the driving force behind this wildly successful business that draws customers from all over the greater Nashville area?

Fay Davidson started looking for a site in 1994. Her goal was to have a place where women could gather and relax around a cup of tea. She did her homework by attending professional seminars on beginning a tea business.

Fay was drawn to a neglected West College Street neighborhood that needed attention. After restoring a building for a gift shop and calling it Nana's Attic, she set her sights on a vacant 100-year-old house sitting across the street, the ideal setting for the tea room. It would be a year before Fay and her husband, Mark, would finish the extensive renovations needed to bring the neglected building back to its original design and decor. With the entire family's assistance, the goal was accomplished, and the tea room/gift shop began drawing customers from all over the southeastern region of the United States.

Inspiration came from the life of Fay's grandmother, affectionately called Miss Mable, who raised 13 children in the Dickson community. Family tradition said that Mable stood for "Mothers Always Bring a Loving Experience."

Guests first notice the enticing southern porch that wraps around the house. It is filled with white wicker furniture and floral cushions, the perfect retreat for tea guests in the spring before the oppressive heat that accompanies a Tennessee summer. In the driveway sits Miss Mable's PT Cruiser with the inscription "Driving Miss Mable" across the back. On its roof is a gigantic fiberglass red hat, a lure to the countless Red Hat Societies that come calling.

Inside, the decor is an unapologetic combination of Victorian kitsch and southern charm – Grandmother's attic in the best sense. This tea room is a nostalgic playhouse where women may don any of the 400 hats, shawls, or lace gloves covering the walls and chair backs. Lace-covered tables hold mismatched china teacups and silver tea strainers. Boldly patterned wallpaper, antique tables and sideboards, lamps with frilly shades, and tasseled curtains add to the dramatic setting, where patrons become actresses in a play that unfolds throughout the week. It is a place where you could easily lose track of time.

Decorator items, tea accoutrements, and fashions needed for an at-home tea party are scattered throughout the four tea rooms and the second floor gift shops. It is a wonderland that cannot be fully

Fay Davidson has created the perfect southern tea room in an area that loves nostalgic memories of a slower life and simpler times. She has honored the memory of her grandmother by "Always Bringing Loving Experiences" to the guests who enter. Mable would be proud.

appreciated with just one visit. Guests come back again and again.

Fay counts herself fortunate in having a supportive family that works behind the scenes to make Miss Mable's flourish. Sons Joseph and John Michael both help out while her daughter Jennifer helps manage the tea room. Jennifer's husband, Chuck Jones, is the head chef.

Chuck's well-equipped kitchen turns out beautiful soups, quiches, buttermilk scones, shrimp salads, tea sandwiches, and a tempting array of desserts that constantly changes. His signature creme bruleè in a demitasse cup is a traditional favorite.

The afternoon tea menu varies monthly with different themes such as a Gone with the Wind Tea or a Rose Garden Tea. Customers choose from the extensive list of 62 teas before the parade of delicious foods arrives displayed on tiered servers, glass dishes and silver trays. Each item is beautifully prepared and presented. Guests feel as if they are having tea in a friend's home.

Danish Puff

1/2 cup	butter, softened
1 cup	all-purpose flour
2 tablespoons	water

Preheat oven to 350° F.

Cut butter into flour until particles are size of small peas. Sprinkle 2 tablespoons water over mixture and mix with fork until pastry forms a ball. Divide into halves and roll, or pat, each half into 12" x 13" rectangles.

Place on an ungreased cookie sheet 3 inches apart. Set aside.

1 cup	water
1/2 cup	butter
1 teaspoon	almond extract
1 cup	all-purpose flour
3	eggs

In a saucepan, heat butter and water to a rolling boil. Remove from heat and quickly stir in almond extract and flour. Stir vigorously over low heat until mixture forms a ball - about 1 minute. Remove from heat. Add eggs and beat until smooth and glossy.

Spread half the mixture over one of the rectangles and repeat with the other half.

Bake 1 hour or until topping has puffed, turned light brown and crisp.

Remove from oven and allow to cool (topping will shrink and fall, forming the custard top). Drizzle sugar glaze over each and sprinkle with nuts if desired.

Sugar Glaze

1 1/2 cups	confectioners' sugar
2 tablespoons	butter, softened
1 1/2 teaspoons	vanilla
	warm water

In a mixing bowl, combine all ingredients. Stir in warm water, 1 teaspoon at a time, until desired consistency is achieved.

Miss Mable's Cookie Jar Tea Cakes

2/3 cup	shortening
3/4 cup	sugar
1	egg
1/2 teaspoon	vanilla
1/2 teaspoon	salt
2 cups	all-purpose flour, sifted
1 1/2 teaspoons	baking powder
2 tablespoons	milk

Preheat oven to 375° F. Cream shortening and sugar. Add egg. Beat mixture until light and fluffy. Add vanilla.

Sift together dry ingredients and stir into creamed mixture along with milk. Divide dough in half and chill for 1 hour. Roll dough out to 1/8 inch. Cut with a favorite cookie cutter.

Place on a greased cookie sheet and bake for about 10 minutes or until light brown.

Makes about 2 dozen medium tea cakes.

LADY MENDL'S

The Inn at Irving
New York, New York

Manhattan Island's early residents possessed an unquenchable thirst for English tea. The colonists' desire for the precious beverage and King George's subsequent taxes eventually brought them to break their bonds with the monarchy. Early New Yorkers loved tea so much that they erected several "tea water pumps" over fresh water springs in lower Manhattan. The clear, bubbling water kept the kitchen kettles full. The springs were located in the vicinity of Christopher Street and at Fourteenth Street and Tenth Avenue. Peddlers of tea-water paraded their carts along the cobbled streets supplying the precious liquid to homes as far north as mid-Manhattan. Over 250 years later, tea is still a precious commodity there.

Gramercy Park is one of four squares laid out by real estate developers in the 19th century to emulate the quiet, private residential areas in many European cities. The townhouses around the square were designed by some of the city's best architects and occupied by its most prominent citizens. Teddy Roosevelt was born just a block away on East 20th Street. Exclusive residences and clubs remain around New York's last private park. Only those who live on the square have an entrance key to the fenced oasis. A stroll south from the park, down Irving Place, leads to East 19th Street, known as "The Block Beautiful." This handsome tree-lined stretch of restored 1920 residences is a block from Pete's Tavern. Since 1903, this cozy neighborhood pub has welcomed thirsty guests, including O. Henry who wrote *The Gift of the Magi* in the second booth.

The next block is home to one of New York's premier boutique hotels and tea rooms, The Inn at Irving and Lady Mendl's Tea Salon. Guests have to look closely for the location. The name is not posted on the townhouse and only a discreet brass plaque bears the name "Lady Mendl's." Its quiet anonymity is what brings many of its customers and celebrity guests back again and again.

Two 1834 landmark townhouses have been meticulously transformed to recreate a bygone era of gracious living. The 12 guest rooms and suites are furnished with exquisite antiques reminiscent of Edith Wharton's New York. Each room bears the name of an interesting local personality from the early 20th century Gramercy Park neighborhood.

Lady Mendl's Tea Salon is named for Elsie DeWolfe, a flamboyant socialite/designer who once lived across the street. She married Lord Mendl, giving her the convenient title of Lady Mendl. She loved tea but not the Victorian fluff that went with it. She was known for bringing homes up-to-date by tearing off heavy Victorian wallpapers and covering walls with the clean look of paint.

Lady Mendl's has a romantic old-world atmosphere. The tall first floor rooms are highlighted by antique lamps, classic chandeliers and soft sunlight filtering through the wood-shuttered windows. Small, intimate tables are scattered throughout the two rooms. Guests also may sit at sofas placed before the fireplace. Several tables are joined to accommodate parties while another private dining room is available for large groups. This is one of New York's most fashionable settings for bridal teas, and the room stays booked months in advance.

The five-course tea meal begins with a light salad followed by a quartet of tea sandwiches - smoked salmon with crème fraiche, cucumber with creamery butter, goat cheese with sun dried tomato, and smoked turkey. Scones with Devonshire cream and preserves come next. The dessert course consists of several tempting cakes - chocolate, lemon, or carrot, to name a few. The meal ends with a selection of beautiful petit fours. The service is efficient without being pretentious.

Afternoon tea at Lady Mendl's is a memorable event. The leisurely meal is never rushed. These are comfortable rooms reminiscent of a quiet Parisian hotel where old friends chat for hours and couples, caught in the sweetness of the moment, lose track of time. After all, it is difficult to think about looking at your watch while cradling a fragrant cup of Darjeeling in your hands.

Madeleines

1 1/4 cups	sifted cake flour
1/2 teaspoon	baking powder
1/4 teaspoon	salt
3	eggs
2/3 cup	sugar
1 teaspoon	vanilla
2 teaspoons	lemon rind, finely grated
3/4 cup	unsalted butter, melted and cooled
	confectioners' sugar for dusting

Preheat oven to 350° F. Sift together flour, baking powder, and salt.

Beat eggs until light. Add vanilla and gradually beat in the sugar, a little at a time. Continue beating until volume has increased about four times the original. Fold in lemon rind. Gradually fold in flour mixture. Stir in the melted, but cool, butter.

Brush pans with additional melted butter. Spoon 1 tablespoon batter into each shell to about 3/4 full. Bake for 12-15 minutes or until golden brown. Remove from pan and dust with confectioners' sugar.

Lemon Cake

1/2 cup	butter
1 cup	sugar
2	eggs
1 1/2 cups	all-purpose flour
1 teaspoon	baking powder
	pinch of salt
1 cup	milk
1	lemon, juice and grated rind

Preheat oven to 300° F. Cream butter and sugar. Add eggs. Sift together flour, baking powder, and salt. Add to butter mixture, alternately with the milk. Mix well. Add lemon juice and grated rind. Bake in a greased loaf pan for 1 hour and 10 minutes.

Lemon Glaze

1/2	lemon
1/4 cup	confectioners' sugar

Juice the half lemon and mix with sugar. Add more juice if needed. Pierce the top of the cake in several places. Pour lemon glaze over it. Allow to cool, slice, and serve.

Truffles

1 cup	cream
3 tablespoons	Grand Marnier, Kahlua, or Amaretto
6 ounces	semi-sweet chocolate
6 ounces	sweet chocolate
8 tablespoons	unsalted butter, softened confectioners' sugar unsweetened Dutch process powdered cocoa

Bring cream to a boil and reduce to 1/2 cup. Add liqueur and chocolate. Stir over low heat until chocolate melts. Whisk in soft butter and mix until smooth. Pour into a bowl and refrigerate until firm.

Use a small melon scoop to shape the chocolate mixture into balls. Roll half of each ball in confectioners' sugar and half in cocoa. Line a covered tin or plastic container with wax paper and store truffles in refrigerator. Makes 50.

SAMOVAR TEA LOUNGE

San Francisco, California

There is a whiff of the exotic when you enter the Samovar Tea Lounge. If your idea of a tea room is a pink cottage filled with frilly Victorian tables and chintz teapots, you are in for a surprise. This is not your grandmother's tea room! Considering the history of tea in this maritime city, it was only a matter of time before the idea of a pan-Asian tea room came to the mind of Jesse Jacobs, and Samovar Tea Lounge was born.

Strategically located on a street corner between the Mission and Castro districts, Samovar is a prime example of how tea is putting on a new face in America. You won't find ladies in hats drinking raspberry tea and eating crustless finger sandwiches here. What you will find is a mix of young professionals, college students and neighborhood regulars who drop by every day to enjoy a pot of tea and a bento box while catching up with the lives of their fellow tea friends. The convivial spirit of this tea sanctuary causes a pause in a busy day. Customers often linger for hours as the gentle morning sunshine streams through the wall of windows and onto their backs.

Everyone knows a samovar is an Eastern European boiler that heats water for tea. Drinking tea around a samovar with friends leads to a warm and comforting environment. Samovar Tea Lounge is founded on that tradition of relaxation and social intimacy. For modern San Franciscans, Samovar is a soothing alternative to noisy liquor bars where friends gather to socialize.

A working samovar sits at the center of the restaurant puffing steam across the teacup-laden bar. Intimate two-seat tables fill the room. A raised platform draws attention to the end of the sunshine-filled café where a long wooden table is placed so that eight to ten guests can sit on straw mats. A 400-year-old statue of Bodhisattva Kuan Yin presides over the gathering. For private parties, a gauzy curtain wraps around the guests like a temple veil.

The emphasis here is on tea. Where else can you find an offering of nine pu-erhs, each with the vintage year listed on the menu? Green, oolong and herbal teas are the most popular choices. Sure, black teas are listed but customers are more into orange ginger than Earl Grey. A variety of Asian teapots and tea bowls stand ready to brew leaves in a variety of ways.

Such a stunning collection of teas can only be paired with equally fascinating foods. Samovar serves beautiful dishes, often involving tea in their preparation. Guests may munch on a small bowl of the green tea-dusted pumpkin seeds or a piece of Karter's Toffee as they sip a cup of Kukicha or Keemun Hao Ya.

One popular dish is Zuke, a tea soup. A pot of green tea is served along with a bowl filled with Napa cabbage, oolong rice and seaweed. Pour the tea into the bowl and your meal is served.

For a bit of Russian flavor, try the Odessa Platter. It includes smoked trout, caviar, red onion, chopped egg, and rye crackers. The menu also offers a selection of small plates, similar to tapas. These might include an artichoke tart, wild salmon tea toasts or lapsang tuna skewers.

And of course there's High Tea served in various fashions: English High Tea, Japanese High Tea, Russian High Tea or Moorish High Tea. Each comes with the sweets, savories, and traditions associated with the culture.

The mission of Samovar Tea Lounge is to bring cultures together into a new concept that captures the essence of international tea traditions in a contemporary way. The owners believe that as more people experience the tea lifestyle, the world will become a better place. Here, the 5000 year tradition of tea has never been fresher.

Miso Pumpkin Soup

4 quarts	hot water
3	parsnips, peeled & diced
1	large sweet potato, peeled & diced
13 ounces	yellow miso
5 cups	pureed pumpkin
1 3-inch sheet	kombu (seaweed)
3 tablespoons	fresh ginger, grated
1 cup	mirin (Japanese cooking wine)
1/4 cup	soy sauce
	scallions, chopped for garnish
	ground nutmeg

In a medium saucepan, bring 1 quart of water to boil. Add parsnips and potatoes and bring to boil again for 15 minutes.

In a small saucepan, soak the kombu in hot water for about 5 minutes.

In a large soup pot, combine 3 quarts of water, miso and pumpkin. Adjust heat to low setting.

Drain potatoes and add to soup. Add kombu, ginger, mirin, and soy sauce. Simmer for 30 minutes.

Pour into individual bowls and garnish with scallions and a dash of nutmeg.

Tea Seared Tuna

1 cup	hojicha (roasted Japanese green tea)
1 tablespoon	kosher or sea salt
1/2 tablespoon	coarsely ground black pepper
4 - 6	ahi tuna fillets
1/3 cup	canola oil
1 tablespoon	sesame oil

In a food processor, prepare the tea rub by blending tea, salt and pepper. Mixture should be coarse.

Soak tuna fillets in ice cold water for 2 to 3 minutes. Remove from water and pat dry with a paper towel. Coat each fillet with tea rub.

In a skillet, heat oils until sizzling. Sear fillets for 2 to 3 minutes on each side. Remove from heat. Slice thin for serving with wasabi mayonnaise.

This dish can be made in advance and served cold. Do not slice until ready to serve or the tuna will dry out.

Wasabi Mayonnaise

1 tablespoon	dry wasabi powder
1 cup	mayonnaise
1 teaspoon	water

Wisk all ingredients together in a small bowl. Serve as an accompaniment to the sliced tuna.

Bergamot Bread Pudding

1	lemon or Seville sour orange
2 cups	milk
5 tablespoons	Earl Grey tea, loose leaf
5 cups	bread cubes
1/2 cup	golden raisins
1 cup	raw sugar
1 tablespoons	nutmeg
3	eggs
	chopped walnuts
	honey

Preheat oven to 375° F. Using a grater, remove zest from the lemon.

In a sauce pan, slowly heat milk to below boil. Add tea to milk and brew for 4 minutes. Strain tea leaves from milk.

In a large mixing bowl, place bread cubes and golden raisins. Add tea-milk and mix lightly with a wooden spoon. Add zest, sugar, and nutmeg. Mix gently and set aside.

In small bowl beat the eggs. Add eggs to the bread mixture and mix together thoroughly.

Coat a bundt pan with butter. Pour in mixture. Place in oven on a tray with a small amount of water. Bake 40-50 minutes.

Spoon warm into serving bowls and top with walnuts and drizzled honey.

Chicken Bombay Sandwiches

2 cups	chicken breast, cooked and slivered
1/2 cup	bacon, cooked and minced
3/4 cup	white cheddar cheese, grated
1/4 cup	red bell pepper, chopped
2 tablespoons	green onions, minced
	salt and pepper to taste
1 teaspoon	garlic, chopped
1 1/2 cup	mayonnaise
dash	Tabasco
1 1/2 tablespoons	curry powder
1/2 teaspoon	ground turmeric
1 package	pita bread

In a large bowl, combine chicken, bacon, cheese, red pepper, and onion. Toss together. Add salt, pepper, curry powder, turmeric, Tabasco, and garlic. Add mayonnaise until desired consistency is achieved.

Toast pita bread. Place chicken spread on pita triangles. Garnish with grapes.

MAGNOLIA & IVY

Sandestin, Florida

America's growing love affair with tea rooms can be traced to a few key gifted entrepreneurs who have faithfully encouraged dreamers to create tea rooms in their own home towns, no matter how small or out-of-the-way. No one in the South has been more influential than two determined sisters from the vicinity of Plains, Georgia.

In an area known for peanuts and cotton, Terri Eager and Kay Snipes crafted four uniquely southern tea rooms in 1995-96. Their tea room/gift shops were housed in former banks and stores. The buildings overflowed with nostalgic touches. Old letters, postcards, photographs, vintage hats, gloves and furs gave diners the feeling of being at grandma's house for a feminine tea party. Cast-off bridesmaid's dresses were kept in a closet for little girls to play dress-up. The shop walls and antique display cases were brimming with every gift and accessory needed to have a home tea party.

The sisters' gracious family members often filled in as chefs and servers. They sometimes dressed as Rhett Butler and Miss Scarlett as they greeted arriving customers. It was a great unapologetic mixture of Margaret Mitchell, Queen Victoria and Martha Stewart. You may have entered as a stranger but you always left with the feeling of being part of their generous extended family. People came from everywhere to see the biggest local attraction since Jimmy Carter.

The Magnolia & Ivy-style tea experience was like nothing else offered in Georgia. In a state where sweet iced tea flowed like water, Terri and Kay poured pot after pot of exotic hot teas from India, China and Sri Lanka. Their foods were handmade and delicious. Tiny finger sandwiches were tied with ribbon like gifts waiting to opened. It wasn't long before this tea party was being duplicated in tea rooms from Florida to California. If you enter any tea room in America and see hats on the wall and furs draped over the chairs, you almost can be assured that the owner has visited "the sisters."

Their success soon came to the attention of the developers of one of Florida's biggest resorts. Sandestin long has been a golfer's paradise and a beach lover's dream. The newly-created village of Baytowne Wharf in the Intrawest Sandestin Development needed an authentic tea room to add to its eclectic mix of upscale restaurants and boutiques. The sisters saw an opportunity to consolidate their enterprises and spread the "good news of tea" to an even larger audience. They left one tea room open in Richland, Georgia and moved their tea business and families from the red clay of Georgia to the white sand of Florida's panhandle.

The new Magnolia & Ivy at Baytowne Wharf is housed off a New Orleans-style brick courtyard, complete with French balconies and gas lights. Guests enter a reception area lined with row after row of tea canisters holding teas from around the world. The main dining room has all the features of a traditional Southern mansion - high ceiling, oversize crystal chandelier and cascading drapes that land in a puddle of color. This fanciful room is reserved for their famous afternoon tea, presented on three-tiered servers and including freshly-baked scones, beautiful finger sandwiches and handmade sweets. A lengthy tea list offers something for everyone's taste in teas.

A retail area is filled from floor to ceiling with teapots, tea wares, books, Victorian knick-knacks, dishes, silver and every tea accoutrement available. It is here that the sisters have added a modern touch to their tea mix - a sleek marble tea bar where tea barristers dispense smoothie tea-based beverages along with nutracueticals, bubble teas, chai, rooibos, and yerba mate. Customers desiring a dessert or lighter fair can be accommodated in the bar area or at a sunny courtyard table. The shop is open for morning, afternoon or evening tea respites.

The entire Magnolia & Ivy concept is based on the customer being "queen." It is a place where your needs are eagerly indulged. The sisters have added a sweet touch to a perfect resort experience, and made a lasting impression on America's tea culture.

White Chocolate Dotted Swiss Cake

2 1/4 cups	sifted cake flour
1 3/4 cups	sugar
1 tablespoon	baking powder
pinch	salt
1/2 cup	vegetable oil
5 large	egg yolks
1 tablespoon	grated orange zest
3/4 cup	water
1 tablespoon	vanilla
5	egg whites
1/2 teaspoon	cream of tartar
1 cup	sugar
1 cup	water
1/4 cup	amaretto
1/2 pint	heavy whipping cream
3 cups	white chocolate, small chunks
1 jar	raspberry jam

Preheat oven to 325° F. Sift flour, sugar, baking powder and salt into mixing bowl. Make a well in center of dry ingredients. Add oil, egg yolks, orange zest and vanilla. Add water 1/4 cup at a time. Beat by hand until batter is smooth and free of lumps.

Earl Grey Crème Brûlée

1 1/2 quarts	heavy cream
5	whole large eggs, slightly beaten
5	large egg yolks, slightly beaten
1 1/2 cups	brown sugar
1 cup	white sugar
1 cup	Earl Grey tea, strongly brewed

Preheat oven to 350° F.

Place heavy cream, slightly beaten eggs, egg yolks, and sugars in top of double boiler. Cook over medium heat, stirring frequently until slightly thickened. Add tea and pour into small ramekins. Bake until set, approximately 50 - 60 minutes. Custard is done when knife stuck in center comes out clean. Cool to room temperature and refrigerate overnight.

Mix a small amount of brown sugar and white sugar together. Pat lightly on top of custard and then torch until sugar melts. Serve immediately.

Key West Poached Salmon

1 1/4 pounds	fresh salmon filet, skin attached
1 1/2 cups	key lime vinaigrette (purchased)
	dried dill
1 1/2 teaspoon	cornstarch
1 tablespoon	sugar
	salad greens

Place salmon filet in glass dish and spoon 1/2 cup of key lime vinaigrette over filet. Marinate for at least one hour. Preheat oven to 350° F. Wrap marinated salmon in a foil pouch and bake for approximately 20 minutes. Salmon is done when it flakes easily. Sprinkle lightly with dried dill. Add cornstarch and sugar to remaining key lime vinaigrette. Heat in small sauce pan until slightly thickened. Pour over salmon, and bake uncovered for 5 minutes. This glazes the salmon. Refrigerate until completely cold. Cut into equal wedges. Remove skin. Place over greens and garnish as desired. Serve with key lime vinaigrette.

Beat egg whites and cream of tartar in separate bowl until very stiff. Gently fold into batter. Do not stir. Line three 6 x 2-inch baking pans with parchment paper. Fill each baking pan 3/4 full. Bake for 50 minutes or until tooth pick stuck in center comes out clean. Cool. Using metal spatula go around rim of cake and loosen cake. Turn out and refrigerate at least 2 hours.

Make ganache by heating whipping cream just to the boiling point. Add chopped chocolate and whip until well blended and smooth. Refrigerate until mixture holds its shape and spreads easily. Make simple syrup with 1 cup of sugar and 1 cup of water. Bring to a boil for 5 minutes. Add amaretto.

Assemble cake by horizontally cutting only two layers in half. (Reserve third layer for another use.) Drizzle simple syrup generously over layers, do not soak.

Spread first layer with a little raspberry jam and repeat until all layers are stacked and have jam between layers. Frost cake with chocolate ganache. Use remaining ganache in pastry bag with a #4 tip and make dots over all edges of cake. Decorate with flowers as desired.

THE MCCHARLES HOUSE

Tustin, California

The correct time for tea depends on your time zone. In England, tea is generally served in late afternoon while tea rooms across the United States might pour tea as early as 1:00. At McCharles House, tea with all its trimmings, flows morning, noon, and night.

Here, British afternoon tea is served on an American schedule to accommodate a busy Southern California lifestyle. Whether it's 11:00 in the morning or 3:00 in the afternoon, tea is being served in Tustin.

For owners Audrey and Vivian Herdia, it took a bit of daring and a large dose of optimism to purchase their shingled Victorian cottage in 1979. Two years of hard work brought the historic landmark, tucked into a side street in Old Town Tustin, back to life. After years of neglect, the home has found a new purpose as it welcomes eager guests underneath its rose-covered trellises and across its well-worn threshold. Thanks to the passion this creative mother-daughter team bring to their vocation, the spirit of McCharles House, named for the family who built it in 1885, has never been stronger.

The mixing bowls in the McCharles House kitchen are filled with an eclectic blend of German, Swedish, and Mexican recipes. Before each new season, Vivian pores over her cookbook collection with a master's intent, crafting menus incorporating many of the flowers and herbs growing in her gardens. The edges on some pages are tattered from use. A ribbon, a postcard, or whatever was handy serve as bookmarks. In the margins are handwritten notes from her "Grammy" with remarks or changes made to enhance the recipe.

Vivian often reads the recipes as if they were a diary. These cookbooks are filled with a lifetime of memories. Holidays, birthdays and special occasions spill from the pages. Grammy jotted down notes for Vivian's first birthday cake. There is a postcard from Aunt Hazel with her delicious chocolate cake. Vivian keeps copious notes on recipe cards as she selects these heirloom recipes to feature in the new menu. She loves to share her memories with her guests.

Born to a family of carpenters and shipbuilders, Audrey always has had an affinity for the craftsmanship and construction of older homes (she admits an enduring love of sawdust and nails). Her artist's eye has transformed this house into a delightful gallery filled with her original paintings. Her sentimental rendition of the tearoom is featured on every tin of McCharles House Tea sold from the gift shop.

The women's creative pallets have spilled over into the gardens where tea-takers dine surrounded by climbing roses, colorful perennials and well-manicured herb gardens. The sight of this fanciful cottage often brings traffic to a halt as motorists crane their necks to see what lies beyond the enchanted walkway. A colorful storybook cottage awaits those who venture in for tea.

Entering the cozy rooms of the bungalow gives the feeling of entering someone's home. Antique tables and chairs, crotchet table cloths, frilly lamps and family photographs fill each room. Antique teacups and teapots line the walls. Lace draped windows look out into the gardens and filter the warm California sunshine. This is a place where guests easily relax, conversations abound, and spirits are refreshed.

Every delicious treat arrives at the table as a work of art. Cakes are colorfully adorned with pansies from the garden, sprigs of rosemary highlight trimmed tea sandwiches, and warm scones come accompanied by fresh strawberry jam and cream. The ever-changing menu keeps guests coming back.

Located south of Anaheim, Tustin is easily accessible from Disneyland, the Nixon Library at Yorba Linda, or the historic Mission of San Juan Capistrano. A visit to The McCharles House should be on the itinerary of every tea loving tourist who visits Southern California. Taking tea in Tustin, anytime of day, will send you home with a sweet memory.

Amelia's Banana Cake

4 tablespoons	unsalted butter
1 1/2 cups	sugar
2	large eggs
1 cup	lightly mashed ripe bananas
1 1/4 cups	unbleached flour
1 cup	whole wheat flour
1/2 teaspoon	salt
3/4 teaspoon	baking soda
1/2 teaspoon	baking powder
1/4 cup	buttermilk
1 teaspoon	vanilla

Preheat oven to 350°F.

In a bowl, with an electric mixer, cream the butter and sugar until light. Add the eggs, one at a time, and beat until combined well. Add the bananas and continue to beat just until combined.

In another bowl, sift the flours, salt, baking soda, and baking powder. Add to the butter mixture, stirring until just combined. Add the buttermilk and vanilla and stir until combined well.

Divide the batter between two well-buttered, floured 9-inch cake pans. Bake for 25 to 30 minutes or until a cake tester inserted in the center comes out clean. Let layers cool in pans on racks for 10 minutes, then invert onto racks and let cool completely.

Frosting

3 cups	confectioners' sugar
6 tablespoons	unsalted butter, softened
1/8 teaspoon	salt
1/2 cup	mashed bananas
1 teaspoon	lemon juice
1/2 teaspoon	vanilla
1 to 2	bananas, sliced thick toasted walnut halves

In a bowl, combine the sugar, butter, and salt. Beat until smooth. In another bowl, combine the mashed banana, lemon juice, and vanilla. Add the banana mixture to the sugar mixture and combine well, adding more sugar if necessary.

Place 1 cake layer on a serving plate, frost with the banana butter cream and top with banana slices. Place second layer on top of banana slices and frost top with remaining banana butter cream. Garnish with toasted walnut halves.

Chocolate Trifle Lorraine

4 ounces	unsweetened baking chocolate, broken into pieces
4 tablespoons	unsalted butter, softened
1 2/3 cups	boiling water
2 1/3 cups	unbleached flour
2 cups	sugar
1/2 cup	sour cream
2	large eggs
2 teaspoons	baking soda
1 teaspoon	salt
1 teaspoon	vanilla

Preheat the oven to 350°F. Butter and flour a 13 x 9 x 2-inch cake pan.

In a bowl, combine the chocolate, butter, and boiling water. Stir until smooth. With an electric mixer set on low speed, add the remaining ingredients until just combined. Do not over beat.

Pour batter into prepared cake pan and bake for 40 to 50 minutes or until a cake tester inserted in the center comes out clean. Let cake cool in the pan on a rack for 10 minutes. Invert the cake on the rack and let cool completely. Cut the cake into cubes and let dry at room temperature for a few hours.

Chocolate Fudge

4 tablespoons	unsalted butter (1/2 stick)
1 1/2 cups	chocolate chips
3/4 cup	heavy cream
2 1/2 cups	sifted confectioners' sugar
1 teaspoon	vanilla

In a saucepan set over low heat, combine all the ingredients and whisk until smooth. Keep warm.

Filling and Decoration

1 1/2 cups	raspberry preserves
	fresh raspberries
	heavy cream

In a large clear bowl, arrange 1/3 of the cake cubes in a layer, spread 1/3 of the raspberry preserves over the cake in a thin layer, and drizzle with 1/3 of the fudge.

Repeat process two more times, decoratively swirling fudge over final layer. Chill 4-6 hours. Before serving, decorate the top of the trifle with fresh raspberries. Serve with a pitcher of heavy cream.

Summery Zucchini-Pistachio Tea Bread

1 1/2 cups	all-purpose flour
1 1/2 teaspoons	baking soda
1/4 teaspoon	ground cinnamon
3/4 cup	sugar
2	large eggs
1/2 cup	vegetable oil
1 teaspoon	vanilla
1/2 teaspoon	salt
1 1/2 cups	grated zucchini, squeezed dry
1 1/2 cups	toasted shelled pistachio nuts

Preheat oven to 350°F.

In a bowl, sift together the flour, baking soda, and cinnamon.

In a second bowl, whisk together the sugar, eggs, vegetable oil, vanilla, and salt. Add to the dry ingredients and stir until combined. Fold in the zucchini and nuts.

Transfer the batter to a well-buttered 5x9" loaf pan and bake for 50-60 minutes or until a cake tester inserted in the center comes out clean.

Let cool in the pan on a rack for 10 minutes. Invert on the rack and cool completely.

Frosting

1	large egg white
3/4 cup	sugar
2 1/2 tablespoons	cold water
1/8 teaspoon	cream of tartar
3/4 teaspoon	light corn syrup
1/2 teaspoon	vanilla

In a double boiler set over simmering water, combine all the ingredients except vanilla.

Using a hand mixer, beat the mixture for 7 minutes or until thick and fluffy. Beat in the vanilla.

Frost the top of cake and allow frosting to set before serving.

"Wouldn't it be dreadful to live in a country where they didn't drink tea?"

Noel Coward

ROSE TREE COTTAGE

Pasadena, California

The picture-perfect setting of Pasadena, California has long been home to one of America's great tea treasures. For nearly two decades, The Rose Tree Cottage and owners, Edmund and Mary Fry, have set the standard for serving a proper afternoon tea. This is the venerable English couple that ignited the tea revolution in Southern California.

"When you come to Rose Tree Cottage," says Edmund, "You come to experience a little piece of England and to be transported, if only temporarily, back to a romantic and nostalgic time." Rose Tree Cottage is actually a historical monument, one of five miniature English storybook thatched cottages built in the 1920s. The gardens, courtyard and buildings are covered with roses and are surrounded by emerald green lawns that face the San Gabriel Mountains. The tea room sits just minutes from the Rose Bowl and a mile from the fantastic Huntington Library and Gardens.

The interior is a scene lifted from a Yorkshire country home. One side table is covered with a who's who collection of celebrity photographs featuring the well-known guests, film stars, dignitaries and members of the Royal Family who have found refuge here over the years. The Frys received an accolade from a special guest when His Royal Highness, the Prince of Wales, visited and pronounced the Rose Tree Cottage a "sterling sight."

Tea is served in three rooms: a large sunny side room, a cozy window-filled sunroom and, everyone's favorite, a parlor with an enticing fireplace surrounded by a few small tables and comfortable upholstered chairs. The window table has an appealing view of English roses and California palms seen through lace curtains.

Guests are surrounded by shelf after shelf of British memorabilia and serenaded by the soft melodies of English music from a bygone era. The sound of clinking china cups and saucers mixes with the sweet fragrance of hot scones and fresh roses.

In a setting reminiscent of a Daphne DuMaurier novel, each guest is seated by the ever-attentive proprietor, dressed appropriately in black tails and white gloves. First time visitors soon realize he takes his role as host seriously while effortlessly directing the countless cues that go into this daily drama, but all are quickly put at ease by his affable demeanor and charm. Mr. Fry serves a never-ending pot of his signature English Village Tea, a mellow Ceylon and Indian blend that is perfect for a relaxing experience.

The Frys and their busy staff serve a traditional Full Afternoon Tea featuring a selection of finger sandwiches (prawn, cucumber, and Tipperary cheese), and freshly baked scones with lashings of Devon cream and their own delicious preserves. To complete the bountiful treat there is a selection of sweets, including the famous Rose Tree Cottage shortbread and Sticky Toffee Pudding. Every beautiful morsel is served on Royal Albert China.

Miss Moppet is another hardworking family member. The 'Sole Cat Proprietor' of Rose Tree Cottage is the official greeter. When not napping, she takes her job very seriously. After the first Rose Tree Cottage cat was cat-napped, this regal feline appeared as a tiny calico kitten left in a gift bag with a note that said "We hope she'll make you happy again." That was years ago and Miss Moppet since has made thousands of friends. Her favorite food, of course, is cream from a tea patron's saucer.

The Frys offer everything imaginable for gifts and home accessories from England. This is one of the finest British shops in the Los Angeles area. The colorful cottage is filled to the brim with British tea pots and china. One room has the look of an English grocery, offering nearly 250 flavors of tea, British foods, cookbooks, and a refrigerated display case with scones, sausage rolls, and other baked goods ready to take home.

Edmund and Mary Fry have earned a well-deserved national reputation for offering a proper tea to thirsty Americans. Their passionate devotion to Edmund's British roots has given them a vocation where they share themselves liberally with all who come through the door of their cherished Rose Tree Cottage. Those who live in the vicinity are fortunate to have such a neighbor where they may refresh themselves regularly. It's as convenient as being in England - without the jet lag.

Sticky Toffee Pudding

4 ounces	butter, softened
6 ounces	dark brown sugar
4	eggs, slightly beaten
8 ounces	self-rising flour
1 teaspoon	baking soda
2 tablespoons	strong coffee with some grounds
8 ounces	dates, pitted and chopped
1 cup	boiling water

Preheat oven to 350° F.

Line a 9-inch square or round cake pan with double parchment paper.

In a mixing bowl, mix together the brown sugar and eggs until smooth. Add the eggs a little at a time, mixing thoroughly after each addition.

Fold in the flour (in three sessions) until smooth.

Place the chopped dates in a medium size mixing

bowl. Mix the baking soda and coffee in a separate small bowl. Pour over dates. Add the boiling water. Stir and let cool slightly. Fold into batter until thoroughly blended. Pour into prepared pan.

Bake for 1 1/2 hours or until springy to the touch. Let cool and top with sauce.

Caramel Sauce

8 tablespoons	brown sugar
4 tablespoons	heavy cream
2 tablespoons	butter

In a saucepan, bring ingredients to a boil while stirring.

Pour over cake and put under the broiler until sauce bubbles, no more than ten minutes. Spoon into bowls and top with a dollop of whipped cream if desired.

Strawberry Rhubarb Cake

3 cups	rhubarb
1 cup	strawberries, quartered
2 envelopes	unflavored gelatin
1/2 cup	superfine sugar

Preheat oven to 350° F. Grease a 9x13" baking dish. In a bowl, combine fruit, gelatin and sugar. Set aside.

1/4 cup	all-purpose flour
1/4 cup	sugar
3 tablespoons	butter

In another bowl, cut butter into flour and sugar until crumbly. Set aside.

1 1/2 cups	sugar
1/2 cup	butter
2	eggs
3 cups	cake flour
4 teaspoons	baking powder
pinch	salt
1 cup	milk

Cream butter and sugar until light and fluffy. Add eggs and beat until fully blended. Combine the flour, baking powder and salt. To the creamed mixture add 1/3 of the dry ingredients. Blend well. Add 1/3 of the milk and blend. Repeat with another 1/3 of dry, then milk. When adding the last 1/3 milk, add vanilla. Beat until blended. Pour batter into prepared pan.

Top with the fruit, then the crumble. Bake for 35-40 minutes or until inserted skewer comes out clean. Serve with cream poured over the top or with clotted cream on the side.

Raj Rolls

1/2 cup	white cheddar cheese
1 1/2 cups	cream cheese
1 tablespoon	*Major Grey's Chutney*
	mango slices

Blend the two types of cheese together in a blender or food processor with the chutney. Pipe into a small butter roll or Parkerhouse and top with mango slices.

THE ST. REGIS HOTEL

New York, New York

A slow spin through a golden revolving door encapsulated with Beaux Arts filigree is all it takes to leave the bustle of Fifth Avenue behind. You have entered a serene refuge of a time long past. A man wearing a tails and white gloves disappears around a marble column - the ghost of John Jacob Astor or a St. Regis doorman? Inside the wood paneled elevator, you hear the light tinkle of crystal from the Waterford chandelier. You wonder if you have somehow escaped the modern world.

For nearly a century, The St. Regis has remained a center of New York's civic, business and social life. The hotel was completely restored in 1988. To keep its golden image as one of the world's premier hotels, 2,500 sheets of 22k gold leaf were applied, making it the second largest gold leafing project ever undertaken in the United States. All that glittering gold is illuminated by 6,000 crystal chandeliers and reflected by over three acres of marble and 2,400 decorative mirrors. The opulent interior has the look of a Viennese palace rather than a hotel. Guests are made to feel like royalty with the services of an on-floor butler, on duty 24 hours and waiting to take care of any need.

Completed in 1904, the 18-story building designed by architects Trowbridge and Livingston was the tallest building in the area at the time and a source of wonderment to visitors. It was declared a New York City Landmark 84 years later.

The site of the hotel, at Fifth Avenue and 55th Street, was a residential neighborhood when Colonel John Jacob Astor IV broke ground for it in 1902. He spared no expense in creating a hotel of world class luxury and taste. The hotel cost $5.5 million to construct. It was lavishly furnished with antique tapestries, oriental rugs, and antique Louis XV furniture. A library of 3000 leather-bound, gold-tooled classic and current books was provided for the hotel's guests and cared for by a private librarian. Colonel Astor was accustomed to fine surroundings. After all, he had spent many summers at his parents' Beechwood mansion in Newport, Rhode Island.

Astor wanted to create a hotel where gentlemen and their families could feel as comfortable as they would as guests in a private home; in fact, he frequently used The St. Regis as a place for his personal guests and visiting relatives to stay at his invitation. For their comfort, he introduced such modern conveniences as telephones in every room, a fire alarm system, central heating and an air-cooling system that efficiently predated modern air conditioning and allowed each guest to control the temperature of his room. Mail chutes were installed on each floor, a newsworthy innovation at that time.

One of the hotel's other novel features was a special design "for the disposition of dust and refuse," one of the first central vacuum systems. All maids had to do was plug their vacuum cleaner's hose into sockets situated throughout the hotel.

The St. Regis soon became the center of Manhattan social life and headquarters for the original "400" list, the elite social group chosen by Colonel Astor's mother. This coveted roster of socially acceptable folk was influenced or even drawn up by her.

Colonel Astor died when the Titanic sank in 1912, leaving the St. Regis to his son, Vincent Astor. Feeling he was too immersed in other real estate ventures to devote the necessary time, he quickly sold the hotel to Duke Management (the tobacco Duke family) who in 1927 expanded the hotel to 540 rooms by extending it along East 55th Street.

The hotel's most famous decoration, the King Cole mural, was installed behind the bar in 1932. The puckish mural by Maxfield Parrish had been given to Colonel Astor by the artist and earlier hung over the bar at Astor's Knickerbocker Hotel.

Leading to the bar lies one of the world's most sophisticated rooms for enjoying tea. On a balustraded dais, the Astor Court appears suspended under a pale, frothy sky, encircled by a mythological mural depicting the Greek ideals of peace, harmony and beauty. In colors of white, gold and pink, it is as

confectionery in spirit as the three-course tea offered.

The Court's dozen or so tables cluster around a central statue banked by flowers. Table settings and exquisite linens from Porthault and porcelain from Limoges by way of Tiffany & Company, are exclusive to the hotel. Eighteen choices of tea are presented in silver teapots to the soothing music of a harp. Rock candy sugar sticks, both amber and crystalline, to dip into your tea at whim, add a sweet touch. An array of savory tea sandwiches are served with a selection of beautiful pastries, scones and Devonshire cream. Delicious Champagne, sherries and dessert wines also are available.

The gilt and grandeur of the opulent tea room may appear intimidating at first glance. But New York is a cramped and crowded place. With its high ceilings, comfortable armchairs, soft light and gorgeous flowers, afternoon tea in the Astor Court is the cure for regaining your sanity. Somewhere, cars are honking and cell phones are ringing - but, at least for now, that world can wait. You are having tea with the ghost of Colonel Astor.

Fruit Tarts

2 cups	all-purpose flour
dash	salt
1/2 teaspoon	sugar
1 1/2 sticks	unsalted butter, chilled and chopped
2-3 tablespoons	ice water

In a bowl, combine flour, salt, sugar, and butter. Mix at low speed for about 8 minutes or until mixture is the consistency of fine cornmeal. Add up to 3 tablespoons of water and continue to mix. The pastry will roll from sides of bowl.

Remove pastry to a lightly floured surface and shape into ball. Cover with waxed paper and chill for 30-45 minutes.

Preheat oven to 450° F. Roll chilled dough to 1/8" thickness. Cut circles with a 2-inch cutter and line each muffin cup with a circle. Bake 8 minutes or until golden.

Crème Anglaise Filling

3	egg yolks
1/2 cup	sugar
1 tablespoon	cornstarch
1 cup	milk
1/4 teaspoon	vanilla
	fresh strawberries or raspberries

In a double boiler, heat egg yolks and sugar. Stir constantly with a whisk until the mixture turns to ribbons. Dissolve cornstarch in milk. Add to egg mixture. Add vanilla and mix until thick. Remove from heat and place on ice. Stir until cold. Cover. Fill each tart with Crème Anglaise and top with fruit.

Fruit Glaze

Mix 2 tablespoons red currant jelly and 1 teaspoon water. Use a brush to paint the fruit topping. Chill.

Salmon and Dill Sandwiches

8 ounces	cream cheese, soft
	heavy cream
1 teaspoon	dill weed, fresh or dried
1 loaf	bread, thinly sliced and buttered
16 slices	thin smoked salmon
	fresh dill or parsley

In a bowl, beat cream cheese, then thin with cream. Mix in dill.

Spread the mixture on bread. Add a very thin slice of salmon. Trim crusts, slice into triangles, and garnish with dill or parsley.

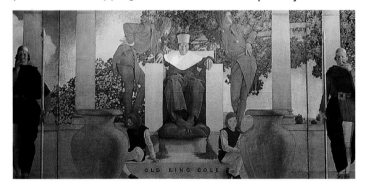

SENTIMENTAL ROSE TEA GARDEN

Longaberger Homestead®
Frazeysburg, Ohio

When the nation's largest manufacturer of hardwood maple baskets decided to build its own turn-of-the-century village east of Columbus, Ohio, the obvious choice for the heart of Longaberger Homestead® was a Victorian tea room. After all, customers who buy thousands of prized Longaberger Baskets® each year are often tea lovers themselves.

The rambling two-story Sentimental Rose Tea Garden resembles a 100-year-old farm home with its welcoming wrap-around porch and neatly manicured rose gardens. One large room, complete with fireplace, accommodates all the dining guests, lending an intimate, comfortable air to tea time.

Longaberger Researcher, Martha Lafferty spent months visiting tea rooms and training her staff before opening the Sentimental Rose Tea Garden in June, 1999. Her hard work paid off because eager guests come from across the country to enjoy a cup of traditional Longaberger® hospitality.

Suzy Foster, Sentimental Rose Tea Garden Manager takes her mission seriously. The skirted tables are set in a Victorian styling with rose-covered English china, whimsical napkin rings, and doilies lining every dish, cup, glass and goblet.

A hot or cold soup course often begins this English ritual while guests look over the wide variety of teas offered, freshly-brewed for each person. The house favorite is *Homestead Blend*, a classic blend of Indian and Chinese black teas with a hint of Lapsang Souchong. Flower-laden three-tiered servers are presented at each table bearing beautiful tea sandwiches, scones, chocolate-dipped fruits, and assorted sweets. The menu changes seasonally so customers are tempted to come back again and again.

Of course, a well-stocked gift area allows the satisfied guest an opportunity to buy Homestead teas, china, silverware, books, and other tea wares so that the tea ceremony might continue at home.

Longaberger Homestead is a patch of America's heartland designed to remind us of a time when families had more time to spend together doing the simple things. This basket empire began with the hard work and vision of the late Dave Longaberger. "It was my father's dream to create an entertainment and educational destination that the entire family can enjoy," explains Tami Longaberger, president and CEO of The Longaberger Company.

Longaberger Homestead® does just that. It offers visitors an opportunity to enjoy a leisurely stroll or hear a town square concert, just as their great-grandparents did. One of Ohio's largest vintage horse barns has been relocated and restored here for all to see. Guests are taught to make their own baskets in the stalls where draft horses once stood. The hayloft seats hundreds of hungry visitors for lunch or ice-cream treats.

Located nearby is Longaberger's basketmaking facility where acres of trained artisans turn out as many as 35,000 baskets each day. Workers sign their creations before sending them on their way. A fascinating free tour takes guests through the gigantic complex, giving them an elevated view of the endless assembly floor. The finishing building next door is where completed baskets are stained, handles attached, and boxed for home delivery.

No trip to this basket Mecca would be complete without stopping to see the World's Largest Basket™. It is the Longaberger headquarters located in a seven-story, open atrium building in the shape of a gigantic market basket - complete with two handles. It is impossible to miss, located on the main highway between Newark and Longaberger Homestead®.

For those more recreationally minded, you can schedule a "tee time" at the premier Longaberger Golf Club®, just down the road.

Whether it's weaving a basket or weaving a memory over a cup of tea, Longaberger Homestead® and the Sentimental Rose™ Tea Garden will quench a longing we all have for a more gentle way of life.

Homestead Cookies

1 cup	all-purpose flour
2 cups	rolled oats
1/2 teaspoon	baking powder
1/2 teaspoon	baking soda
1/2 teaspoon	salt
1 cup	apples, chopped fine
1/2 cup	butter, room temperature
1/2 cup	granulated sugar
1/2 cup	light brown sugar
1	egg
1 1/2 teaspoons	vanilla

Preheat oven to 375° F.

Line baking sheets with parchment or grease lightly.

In a large bowl, cream together butter, granulated sugar, and brown sugar until light and fluffy. Beat in egg and vanilla.

In another bowl, stir together flour, oats, baking powder, baking soda, and salt. Gradually mix dry ingredients into butter mixture. Stir in apples.

Drop a tablespoon of dough onto prepared baking sheets, leaving 1 1/2 inches between them.

Bake 8 to 10 minutes or until light golden. Cool on wire racks and store in airtight container.

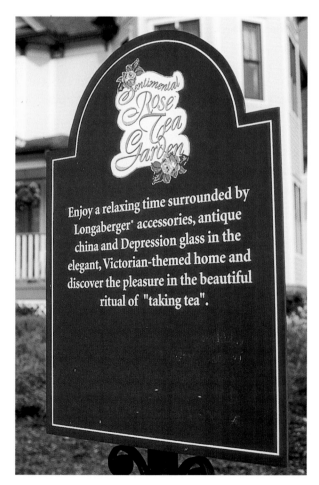

Toffee Bars

4 ounces	butter, room temperature
4 ounces	light brown sugar
1	egg yolk
1/3 cup	all-purpose flour
1 cup	oats

Preheat oven to 375° F. Grease a 7x11-inch Swiss roll or tart pan. Beat together the butter, sugar, and egg yolk until light and smooth. Add the flour and oats, mix well. Press into the prepared pan and bake for 15-20 minutes or until lightly browned. Remove from the oven and cool slightly in the pan.

Topping

3 ounces	chocolate
1 ounce	butter
1 cup	chopped walnuts or almonds

In a pan, melt together the chocolate and butter. Spread over the warm cake. Top with nuts and allow topping to set. While still warm, cut into bars and allow to completely cool before storing in an air-tight container.

Cranberry Bars

1/4 cup	butter, room temperature
1/4 cup	brown sugar, packed
1/2 cup & 2 Tbsp.	all-purpose flour
1	egg
1/2 cup	granulated sugar
1 1/4 cups	dried cranberries and raisins, mixed
1/2 cup	chopped walnuts
1/2 cup	coconut
2 tablespoons	orange juice or orange liqueur
1 tablespoon	orange zest
1 teaspoon	cinnamon
1/2 teaspoon	vanilla
1/4 teaspoon	salt

Preheat oven to 375° F.

In a mixing bowl, cream butter. Add brown sugar and 1/2 cup flour. Mix into a dough.

Pat dough onto the bottom of an 8" square baking pan. Bake for 5 minutes.

Mix remaining flour with all other ingredients. Spread mixture over hot crust. Return to oven for 25 minutes or until edges are lightly browned. Allow to cool completely before cutting into bars.

THE SWAN HOUSE

Findlay, Ohio

Tea rooms across America are breathing new life into historical buildings by turning often neglected properties into viable businesses. Old mansions, storefronts, cottages, carriage houses, and banks are vibrant again as optimistic entrepreneurs find new missions for these architectural gems. The grand Swan House is one ugly duckling that was gloriously transformed in Findlay, Ohio.

This impressive Victorian Italianate brick mansion was once the home of one of Findlay's best-known families, the Hoslers. Located just a few blocks off the main street, it changed dramatically over the years as it housed a doctor's office, beauty shop, and eventually, seven apartments. Modern "improvements" had taken a toll on the classic beauty of the 125-year-old house. A 1950's front door and porch were hiding the original radius window over the tall double front doors. Ceilings throughout the house had been lowered to conserve heat, and interior doorways had been walled off.

It took the foresight and enthusiasm of local residents Kay Kose, Vicki Powell and Rindy Crates to restore the house to its original splendor. They soon found that they had to stir a lot of dust before they could make tea. The transformation began in 1998 and was completed in just six months.

Ripping out the false ceilings revealed hidden transoms over the doorways. The well-worn wooden floors were refinished to add a warm golden glow to the public rooms. One of the greatest finds was a treasure trove of original interior shutters, neatly numbered and stacked in the attic. The new owners had them stripped, refinished, and re-hung in their original frames. This eliminated the need for window treatments and saved a great deal of money.

These faithful ladies found it easy to settle on a name for their new tea room. The image of a swan stood on top of many Lutheran churches during the Reformation, symbolizing new life. The graceful, elegant creature was the unanimous choice as a name for their fledgling business. Since their grand opening, Renee Chaskel and Nancy Wilch have joined the partnership.

The spacious main dining room seats 25 people in antique chairs around elegant, double-draped tables. A fascinating collection of antique china cups and plates are used for the tea service. The tall double hung windows provide an uninterrupted view of the neighborhood. Two cozy tables beside the windows are perfect to soak up some rare northern Ohio sunshine on a cold winter day.

A quiet brick-walled garden room holds four checker-clothed tables, great for private parties and tea showers. Plates, prints and gifts line the walls.

Two rooms of tea-related gifts await perusing on the first floor while two rooms of antiques and crafts may be found upstairs, along with a guest suite.

The owners have done a great deal of research

Lime Meltaways

3/4 cup	butter, room temperature
1/3 cup	powdered sugar
1 tablespoon	vanilla
2	limes, zested
2 tablespoons	lime juice
1 3/4 cups	all-purpose flour
2 tablespoons	cornstarch
1/4 teaspoon	salt

Cream together butter, powdered sugar and zest.

Sift flour, cornstarch, and salt together.

Combine all ingredients to form a stiff dough.

Form into logs approximately the diameter of a half dollar and freeze.

Slice when needed. Bake for 10-12 minutes in a 350° F oven. Cool and roll in powdered sugar.

while planning their venture. They have attended tea conferences, visited tea rooms across the country, and read countless cookbooks over the past few years. Their attention to detail is evident from the time guests enter the front door. Every room is perfectly decorated with a mix of antiques and appropriate gift wares, mostly based on a tea or swan theme.

A wide selection of loose leaf teas are offered, including a floral Monet's Garden and a Swan House Blend. The owners take turns planning the menus that change monthly. An assorted mix of foods from both English and Midwest cuisines are found here. Tomato and basil tea sandwiches are often served on the tiered server next to a broccoli cheese cornbread or blueberry-stuffed French toast sticks. Of course everyone's favorite is the quintessential swan cream puffs dusted with confectioners' sugar.

Just as the graceful swan epitomizes beauty and elegance, the Swan House has earned a well-deserved regional reputation by offering exceptional charm and gracious hospitality. The energetic owners are fanning the flames of America's new tea revolution by introducing countless guests to the pleasures of a proper afternoon tea.

Sun Dried Tomato and Walnut Potatoes

1 1/2 pounds	red skinned potatoes
15	sun dried tomato halves (not packed in oil)
1 teaspoon	dried rosemary
2 cloves	garlic
1/2 cup	fat free mayonnaise
1/3 cup	cottage cheese
1 tablespoon	lemon juice
3/4 cup	chopped walnuts
	salt & pepper to taste

Steam potatoes. Cool to room temperature and slice in half. Hollow out 1 tablespoon from each center.

Cover tomato halves with boiling water and soak for 10 minutes. Drain and pat dry.

Place in food processor with rosemary and garlic. Process until coarsely chopped. Add the mayonnaise, cottage cheese, and lemon juice. Process until smooth. Add walnuts and process until incorporated. Season with salt and pepper. Yields 1 1/2 cups of tomato filling.

Spoon 1 tablespoon of tomato filling into each potato half. Serve at room temperature.

Summer Corn Pancakes

1 box	Jiffy corn muffin mix
1 cup	sour cream
1 cup	cream style corn
1/3 cup	melted butter
3	whole eggs
4 teaspoons	sugar

Mix all ingredients and beat until smooth. Drop on hot skillet or griddle until lightly browned on both sides.

ALICE'S TEA CUP

New York, New York

Alice may have fallen down a rabbit hole to reach her mad tea party, but you'll only have to step down a short flight of stairs to enter one of New York's most colorful tea rooms. Sisters Haley and Lauren Fox, life-long tea lovers, created a wonderland in the upper West Side where everyone seems to feel welcome.

On any given day, an eclectic group of tea lovers fills the two cozy dining rooms. Mothers with small children, aspiring actors, tourists, and neighborhood regulars gather for conversation and camaraderie over a cup of tea. The Raspberry Room often becomes a private alcove for bachelorette parties, wedding showers, or their famous "un-birthday parties."

The misconception that New Yorkers are hardened and serious falls by the wayside in this land of make-believe. Perhaps guests feel comfortable because the décor is cheerfully casual. Cream-colored walls are decorated with whimsical quotes: *We're all mad here!* and *Teatime is quiet time. Off with your cell phone or off with your head!*

The actors in this outrageous scenario are seated at mismatched wooden tables and chairs or lounging on floral-patterned banquettes. Aspiring "Alices" may choose from a selection of colorful party dresses that await them as they make their way through the narrow hallway.

Although the atmosphere may seem playful and carefree, the owners are serious about their tea. Guests may choose from 120 types of loose tea. All teas are brewed in double-filtered water and served in a china pot, equipped with a decorative sponge drip-catcher.

Several set teas are offered. The combinations all have whimsical names such as *The Nibble, The Mad Hatter, The Jabberwocky,* or *The Wee Tea*. Alice's scones are huge and almost a meal on their own. The flavors change daily with pumpkin being one of the most popular.

The eccentric menu delights your mind even before your physical hunger is satisfied. The menu reads like a fairy book with "sweets and treats for the Alice in all of us." These include such delights as chai crème brulee, mochachocolatechip cake, Verveine tea-infused lemon tart, raspberry-mint tea sorbet, Tahitian vanilla gelato, chocolate mousse, s'mores, mixed berries with homemade Chantilly crème and lavender honey, or a vanilla ice cream sandwich served on a peanutbutterchocolate chip cookie. There is even a daily puree just for babies.

Haley and Lauren spent years traveling to tea rooms around the world, dreaming of the time they would open their own tea house in New York City. Their dream has come true and they have made "Alices" of us all.

Mother Hubbard's Squash Soup

2 large	winter squash
2 medium	yellow onions
1 large	leek
1 tablespoon	garlic
11/2 quarts	chicken stock
1 quart	cream
4 ounces	butter
	salt to taste
	pepper to taste

Split squash and remove seeds. Bake at 350° F until soft (pierces easily with knife). Set aside. Melt 2 ounces butter in sauce pan and sauté onion, leek, and garlic until translucent. Add chicken stock.

Cook until hot. Add squash.

In another pan reduce the cream by half and add to the soup. Add remaining butter to soup and blend in a blender. Season with salt and pepper. Serve hot.

Carrot Cake

2	medium eggs
1 cup	sugar
3/4 cup	oil
1/2 cup	walnuts, finely chopped
1 cup	all-purpose flour, sifted
8 ounces	carrots, grated
1 teaspoon	cinnamon
1 teaspoon	baking soda

Preheat oven to 350° F. Oil and line a 7" round cake tin.

Beat the eggs and sugar together until thick and very pale. Beat in the oil gradually, and then fold in the rest of the cake ingredients using a metal spoon.

Pour into the prepared pan and bake for 45-50 minutes or until firm and a skewer comes out clean when inserted in the center.

Remove from oven and allow to cool in pan for 15 minutes before turning out on wire rack.

Topping

1 1/2 cups	confectioners' sugar
2 ounces	butter, room temperature
3 ounces	cream cheese
1/2 teaspoon	vanilla

Beat all ingredients together until very smooth and fluffy. Spread over top of cake.

Iced Matcha

1 teaspoon	matcha green tea
2 teaspoons	sugar
2/3 cup	190° F water
	ice cubes

Whisk matcha, sugar, and hot water until frothy. Pour into a tall glass of ice.

Green Tea Smoothies

1 1/2 teaspoons	green tea
1 1/2 cups	low fat yogurt
2	medium ripe peaches, pitted and chunked (mangos or apricots may be substituted)
1-3 teaspoons	honey
6	ice cubes

Place all ingredients in a blender and puree until completely blended.

Serve immediately in a tall glass.

Pumpkin Scones

4 1/2 cups	all-purpose flour
5 teaspoons	baking powder
1 teaspoon	cinnamon
1/2 teaspoon	nutmeg
1 teaspoon	salt
1/2 cup	light brown sugar
1/2 cup	unsalted butter, softened
2 cups	canned pumpkin puree
1 1/3 cups	milk
2 cups	pecans, chopped

Preheat oven to 375° F. Prepare two large baking sheets with cooking spray.

In a large mixing bowl, combine dry ingredients. Cut in the butter until it resembles coarse meal. Add pumpkin, milk and nuts. Stir until well mixed. Using a 1/2 cup measure, scoop the batter into small rounds on the baking sheets. Leave a 2" space between each scone. Place the remaining batter in the refrigerator until the first batch has finished baking.

Bake for 12 to 15 minutes, until the edges begin to brown. Remove to a cooling rack. Makes 2 1/2 dozen scones.

108

THE TEA ROOM

Savannah, Georgia

If ever there was an American city that was a perfect location for the enjoyment of afternoon tea, it is the beautiful coastal city of Savannah, Georgia. Hospitality, landscape and architecture all come together in this historic setting to serve as the backdrop for one of the South's finest tea presentations.

The inspiration for The Tea Room of Savannah was sparked a century ago in far-off Glasgow, Scotland. Kate Cranston, a prominent Victorian tea room entrepreneur, commissioned art nouveau artist/architect Charles Rennie Mackintosh to design five tea rooms in the city. They were bold and organic in style. So complete was his vision that he created not only the building, but also the furniture, leaded glass windows, murals, and light fixtures. Even his unique calligraphy was used on the menus and signage. His avant garde creations are well-known today by students of both tea and architecture. Thousands of Mackintosh devotees make the pilgrimage to Glasgow to see his only original tea room still in operation, The Willow Tea Rooms on Sauchiehall Street.

Elizabeth Ruby became a fan of Mackintosh long before she dreamed of opening a tea room with partners Rebecca Wright (her mother), Marjorie Jones, and Gloria Horstman. Her love of Mackintosh's bold designs compelled her to pay homage to his vision in Georgia. Mackintosh and Miss Cranston would be proud to know that The Tea Room of Savannah is one of several newly-restored Broughton Street businesses that are again bringing vitality and loyal customers to this once-bustling retail district.

From the time you walk through the door of The Tea Room, you know you are in a serious tea shop. As is the case at Mariage Freres in Paris or Bettys of York, row after row of tea canisters are the first things you see lining the shelves behind the front counter. Over 60 selections of fine quality teas from around the world await your choosing. Each is precisely brewed for the customer according to water temperature and steeping time. And if you find something you wish to experience again, you may buy a few ounces to take home for your next tea celebration.

Like many who fall victim to the mesmerizing influence of Mackintosh, the owners were inspired to follow their dream of creating a tea room with as many of the artist's touches as they could employ. High-back chairs, low light lamps, antiques, and potted plants all add to the comfortable feeling of this soothing sanctuary. Much of the eclectic mix of china and linens was gathered from the wealth of antique shops in this area.

This is an atmosphere conducive to conversation and lingering afternoons. An inviting fireplace adds a relaxing air to the library dining room, where tea and books could easily convince a guest to spend a few hours. As was the case in Miss Cranston's Scottish tea rooms, the customer here is offered a tempting variety of scones, pastries, soups, sandwiches, and cakes. Each is made fresh daily by chef and newest partner Andre Baxter. Teatime choices range from a simple cream tea to the full afternoon tea served on tiered trays.

After tea, you may want to take a leisurely stroll through Savannah's historic azalea-covered squares. Savannah is best explored by walking. Antebellum mansions, stately churches and moss-draped oaks lie around every turn of the cobblestone streets. Search out familiar movie settings such as the Bonaventure Cemetery from "Midnight in the Garden of Good and Evil" or Forrest Gump's famous park bench. At dusk, walk hand-in-hand along the riverfront and wave at ships going upriver.

These unique features could be the reason General William Tecumseh Sherman could not bring himself to burn this magnificent city on his relentless march to the sea in1863. Instead, he presented it as a Christmas gift to his commander-in-chief, President Lincoln, and one of America's great gems was saved. Thank goodness it was.

Lapsang Souchong Poached Chicken Salad

3 pounds	boneless chicken breast
3 quarts	water
1/4 cup	Lapsang Souchong or orange pekoe tea
1/4 cup	soy sauce
1 ounce	ginger root, chopped
1	large apple, chopped
2	garlic cloves, chopped
2 tablespoons	chopped red bell pepper
2 tablespoons	chopped yellow bell pepper
2 cups	mayonnaise
1/2 teaspoon	salt
1/8 teaspoon	white pepper

Trim any fat from the chicken, cut the chicken into halves. Combine the chicken and enough water to cover in a 5 quart saucepan. Add the tea and soy sauce. Bring to a boil; reduce the heat to just below the boiling point. Poach for 30 minutes or until the chicken is cooked through. Let stand to cool. Drain and rinse the chicken and cut into medium chunks.

Combine the ginger root, apple, garlic, red pepper, and yellow pepper in a bowl. Add the mayonnaise and mix well. Stir in the chicken. Season with salt and white pepper. Serve on toasted wheat bread.

Perkins

2 cups	all-purpose flour
1 1/3 cups	oatmeal
1 cup	sugar
1/2 teaspoon	baking soda
2 1/2 teaspoons	ginger
1/2 teaspoon	nutmeg
1/2 teaspoon	allspice
1/2 teaspoon	cinnamon
4 ounces	butter
1	egg, beaten
6 teaspoons	light corn syrup

Preheat oven to 350° F. Grease a baking sheet. Combine the dry ingredients. With your fingers, work in the butter until it resembles breadcrumbs, or mix in a food processor. Add beaten egg and syrup. Form dough into golf-ball size shapes. Put an almond on each and flatten slightly. Bake about 15 minutes. Makes 30 cookies.

Vanilla Butterscotch Bread

3 cups	all-purpose flour, sifted
1 1/4 teaspoons	double acting baking powder
3/4 teaspoon	salt
3/4 teaspoon	baking soda
2	eggs, beaten
1 1/2 cups	light brown sugar
1/3 cup	butter, melted
1 1/2 teaspoons	vanilla
3/4 cup	chopped nuts
1 1/2 cups	buttermilk

Preheat oven to 350° F. Sift together the first 4 ingredients.

Beat eggs in a mixing bowl. Gradually blend in sugar. Add butter and vanilla. Stir in nuts. Add flour mixture alternately with milk, mixing only enough to blend the ingredients.

Turn into a well-greased, lightly floured 9x5x3-inch loaf pan. Bake 1 hour or until done. Cool in pan 10 minutes. Turn onto a wire rack to finish cooling.

Scotch Whiskey Balls

2 cups	gingersnap cookies, finely ground
1 cup	pecans, finely ground
1/4 cup	Scotch whiskey
3 tablespoons	corn syrup
1 1/2 cups	powdered sugar, sifted

In a mixing bowl, combine cookie crumbs, nuts, whiskey, corn syrup, and 1 cup powdered sugar.

Mix thoroughly with a wooden spoon. Form into small balls. Roll each ball in powdered sugar. Make ahead and chill for future use.

THE WALDORF=ASTORIA

New York, New York

The art deco explosion of the 1930's marked the building of some of New York's most recognized landmarks. The Empire State Building, Rockefeller Center, and the Chrysler Building were all monuments to this streamlined modern era. A fashionable Saturday afternoon in lower Manhattan included shopping along Fifth Avenue, taking in a show at Rockefeller Center and enjoying afternoon tea at the stylish Waldorf-Astoria.

In 1893, millionaire William Waldorf Astor launched the first Waldorf Hotel at Fifth Avenue near 34th Street. In 1897, The Waldorf was joined by The Astoria Hotel, erected on an adjacent site by his cousin, John Jacob Astor IV.

In 1929, after decades of hosting distinguished visitors from around the world, The Waldorf closed its doors to make room for what would become another famous landmark, the Empire State Building.

Thousands of onlookers watched on October 1, 1931 as the new Waldorf=Astoria opened its doors. The mighty 2,200-room hotel stretched all the way from Park Avenue to Lexington Avenue and occupied the entire block from 49th to 50th Streets. From his office in the White House, President Herbert Hoover delivered a message of congratulations on the hotel's opening. After leaving office, he became a permanent resident of the Waldorf Towers.

With the establishment of the United Nations in New York, the Waldorf became the first and only hotel in the world to house an ambassadorial residence. The seal affixed to the door frame of one suite marks it as the home of the United States Ambassador to the U.N.

So many world leaders have curled up for a night in the Waldorf Towers that it has been said only Buckingham Palace has hosted more heads-of-state. An apocryphal story has it that one day a caller phoned The Towers and asked to speak to the king, to which the polite operator replied, "Which king?"

Composer Cole Porter wrote many of his famous lyrics at The Waldorf where he was a resident for 25 years. The Waldorf gave Porter a Steinway grand piano as a gift. The beautiful floral print decorated piano now resides in the Cocktail Terrace in the Park Avenue Lobby, where it is played daily. In his suite, Porter arranged two grand pianos, placed curve to curve. He would often invite his talented friends to the suite for some friendly piano dueling. Frank Sinatra later lived in this suite.

The centerpiece of the hotel lobby is a giant gilded clock with a miniature Statue of Liberty resting on top. Executed for the Chicago World's Fair of 1893, it was brought from the original hotel. "I'll meet you at the clock in the lobby of the Waldorf" is a common phrase for regular guests meeting clients or friends.

The magnificent Park Avenue lobby is the setting for traditional afternoon tea. The lobby has been restored to its original art deco glory with bas-relief friezes and grillwork setting off the beautifully painted murals, deep mahogany paneling, and elegant marble columns. Guest enjoy tea while seated at petite tables perched above the classic mosaic tiled entry. They have an uninterrupted view of the endless spectacle of guests entering and exiting the hotel. It is not unusual to spot a celebrity or visiting diplomat in the crowd. This ceremony, accompanied by music from Cole Porter's piano, plays out as if it was the 1930's again. Delicious sweets and savories, scones with cream and preserves, and a selection of loose leaf teas make this New York experience all the more satisfying.

Tea at the Waldorf has always been a part of many resident New Yorkers' schedules. For out-of-town visitors, this fashionable affair makes a great New York memory to carry home. It could easily become a regular occurrence for tea lovers who enjoy their tea sweetened by great architecture, unforgettable music, and rich tradition.

Pear and Stilton Sandwiches

4 slices	honey-oat bread, thinly sliced
1 tablespoon	butter, room temperature
1	ripe pear, halved and sliced thin
1 tablespoon	fresh lemon juice
2 tablespoons	Stilton cheese, crumbled

Spread each bread slice with the soft butter. Sprinkle lemon juice on the sliced pears. Place half the pear slices in a single layer on a slice of bread. Top with half the crumbled cheese and a second bread slice. Repeat, using all remaining ingredients.

Trim crusts and cut into 8 finger sandwiches.

Macaroons

1/4 cup	confectioners' sugar, sifted
1 cup	powdered sugar
1 cup	ground almonds
3	egg whites
1/8 teaspoon	almond essence
	powdered sugar for dusting
35-40	whole blanched almonds

Preheat oven to 300° F. Line two baking sheets with parchment paper.

In a large bowl, mix sugars and ground almonds. Make a well in the center and drop in one egg white. Using a fork, work the egg white into the sugar mixture until a stiff, smooth paste is formed. Gradually work in the remaining egg whites until the paste is soft and smooth. Add almond flavoring.

Put the mixture into a piping bag fitted with a medium star nozzle. Pipe about 10 small biscuits on each baking sheet. Extra mixture may be refrigerated until ready to cook the next batch. Dust each macaroon with confectioners' sugar and top with an almond. Bake for 30 minutes or until firm and golden.

Remove from oven and slide the parchment paper and macaroons on a wire rack. Leave to cool completely. Re-line the baking sheets and pipe and bake the remaining mixture. When the macaroons are cool, remove them from the paper.

Waldorf Celery Boats

2 stalks	fresh crisp celery
1/2 cup	blue cheese, crumbled
1/4 cup	finely chopped toasted walnuts
1/2 cup	finely chopped red delicious apple
1 teaspoon	lemon juice
	leaf lettuce

Cut celery into 1-1/2 inch bite-size pieces. In a medium bowl, combine blue cheese and walnuts. In a small bowl, mix the lemon juice with the chopped apple. Drain off any excess juice. Add apple to the cheese mixture. Gently mix together. Place a small amount of mixture into each piece of celery. Place each celery boat on top of a piece of leaf lettuce and serve. Serves 16.

THE GREAT TEA ROOMS OF AMERICA

Alice's Tea Cup
102 W. 73rd Street at Columbus Avenue
New York, New York 10023
212.799.3006
www.alicesteacup.com

Brown Palace
321 17th Street
Denver, Colorado 80202
303.297.3111
www.brownpalace.com

Butchart Gardens
800 Benvenuto Avenue
Brentwood Bay, British Columbia V8M 1J8
250.652.8222
www.butchartgardens.com

Cliffside Inn
2 Seaview Avenue
Newport, Rhode Island 02840
401.847.1811
www.cliffsideinn.com

The Drake Hotel
140 East Walton Place at Michigan Avenue
Chicago, Illinois 60611
312.787.2200
www.thedrakehotel.com

The Dunbar House
1 Water Street
Sandwich, Massachusetts 02563
508.833.2485
www.dunbarteashop.com

Boulder Dushanbe Teahouse
1770 13th Street
Boulder, CO 80302
303.442.4993
www.boulderteahouse.com

Fairmont Empress Hotel
721 Government Street
Victoria, British Columbia V8W 1W5
250.389.2727
http://www.fairmont.com/empress

Farmhouse Tea Shoppe
5455 Chamblee Dunwoody Road
Dunwoody, Georgia 30338
770.673.0099
www.farmhouseteashoppe.com

The Grand Floridian at Walt Disney World
4401 Grand Floridian Way
Lake Buena Vista, FL 32830-1000
407.824.3000
www.disney.com

Lady Mendl's
56 Irving Place
New York, New York 10003
212.533.4600
www.innatirving.com

Magnolia & Ivy
Village at Baytowne Wharf
Sandestin, Florida 32550
850.267.2595
www.magnoliaivy.com

McCharles House
335 South C Street
Tustin, California 92780
714.731.4063
www.mccharleshouse.com

Miss Mable's Tea Room
301 West College Street
Dickson, Tennessee 37055
615.441.6658
www.missmable.com

Queen Mary Tea Room
2912 NE 55th Street
Seattle, Washington 98105
206.527.2770
www.queenmarytea.com

Rose Tree Cottage
828 E. California Boulevard
Pasadena, California 91106
626.793.3337
www.rosetreecottage.com

The St. Regis Hotel
Two East 55th Street
New York, New York 10022
212.753.4500
www.stregis.com

Samovar Tea Lounge
498 Sanchez Street at 18th Street
San Francisco, California 94114
415.626.4700
www.samovartealounge.com

Sentimental Rose Tea Room
Longaberger's Homestead Village
5565 Raiders Road
Frazeyburg, Ohio 43822
740.322.5588

Swan House
225 West Sandusky Street
Findlay, Ohio 45840
419.429.7926
www.swanhousetearoom.com

The Tea Room
7 East Broughton Street
Savannah, Georgia 31401
912.239.9690
www.savannahtearoom.com

Waldorf=Astoria
301 Park Avenue
New York, New York 10022
212.355.3000
www.waldorf.com

RECIPE INDEX

"There are few hours in life more agreeable than the hour dedicated to the ceremony known as afternoon tea."

Henry James